impressions

by elaine morrison

first publishing Toronto, Canada 2013

Library and Archives Canada Cataloguing in Publication
Morrison, Elaine, 1968-, author, artist
Impressions / by Elaine Morrison.
ISBN 978-0-9739682-8-6 (pbk.)
    1. Morrison, Elaine, 1968-.
    2. Digital art--Ontario--Toronto.
I. Title.
N7433.85.M67A4 2013   776'.40971354
C2013-908221-2

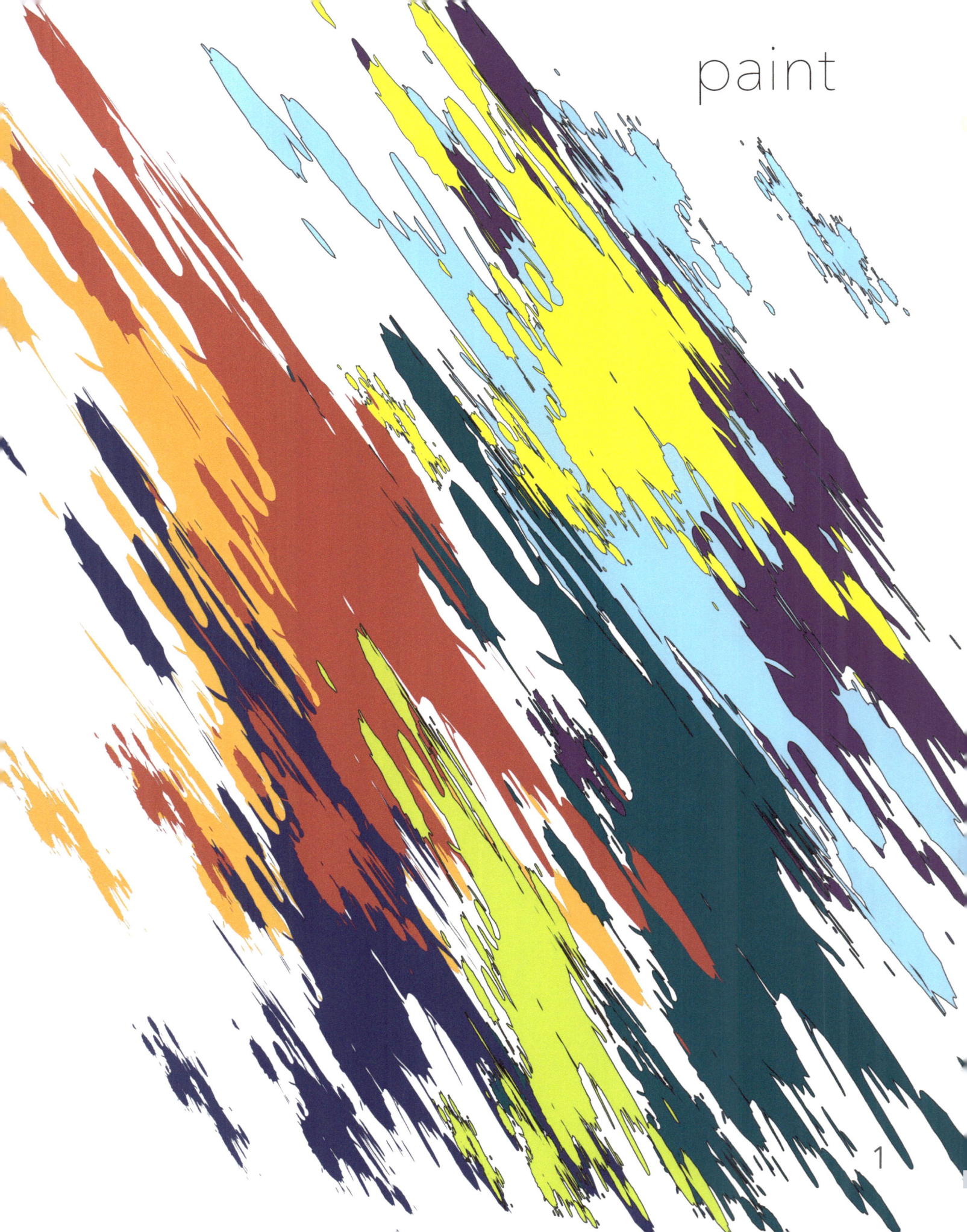

paint

1

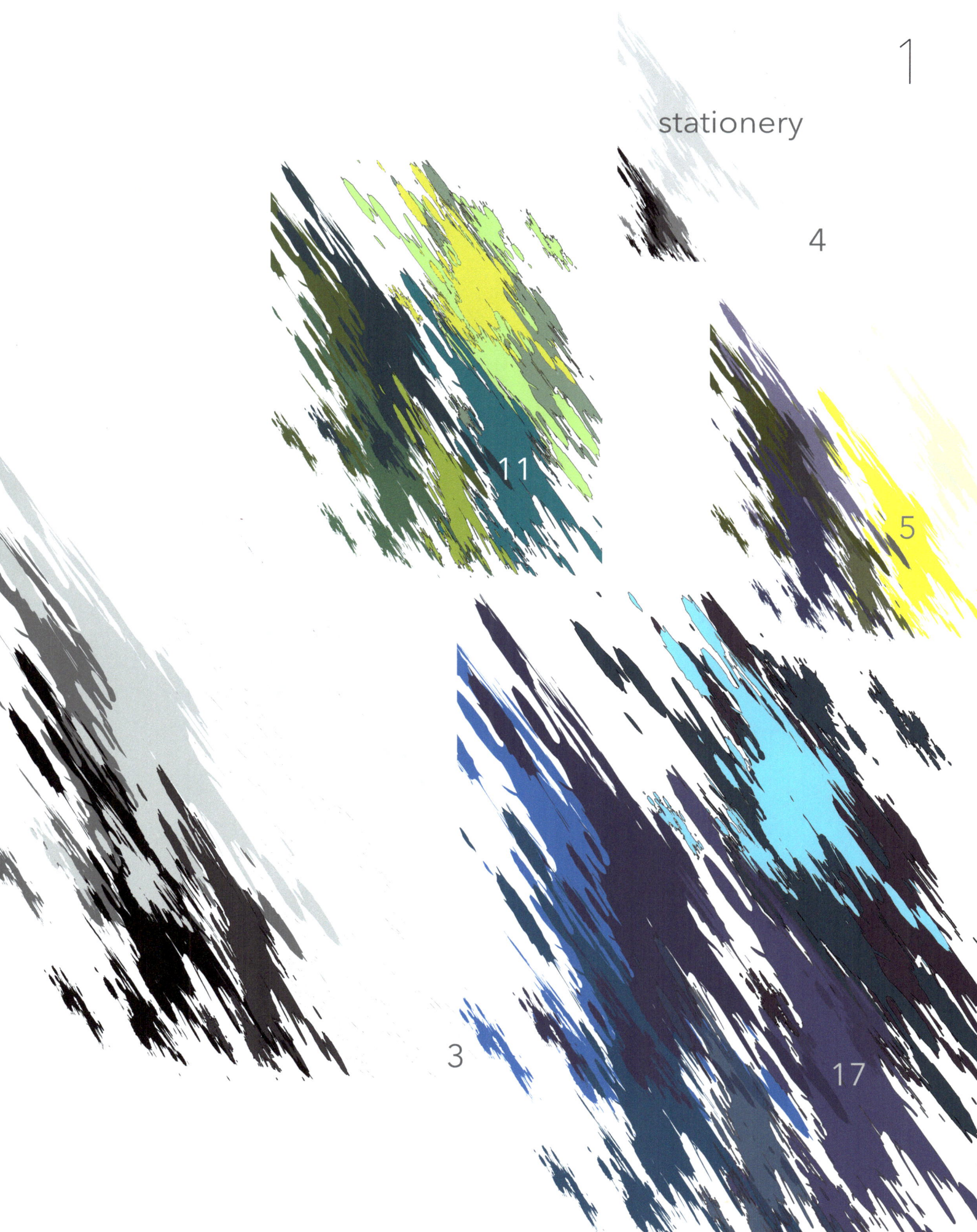

stationery

1

4

5

11

3

17

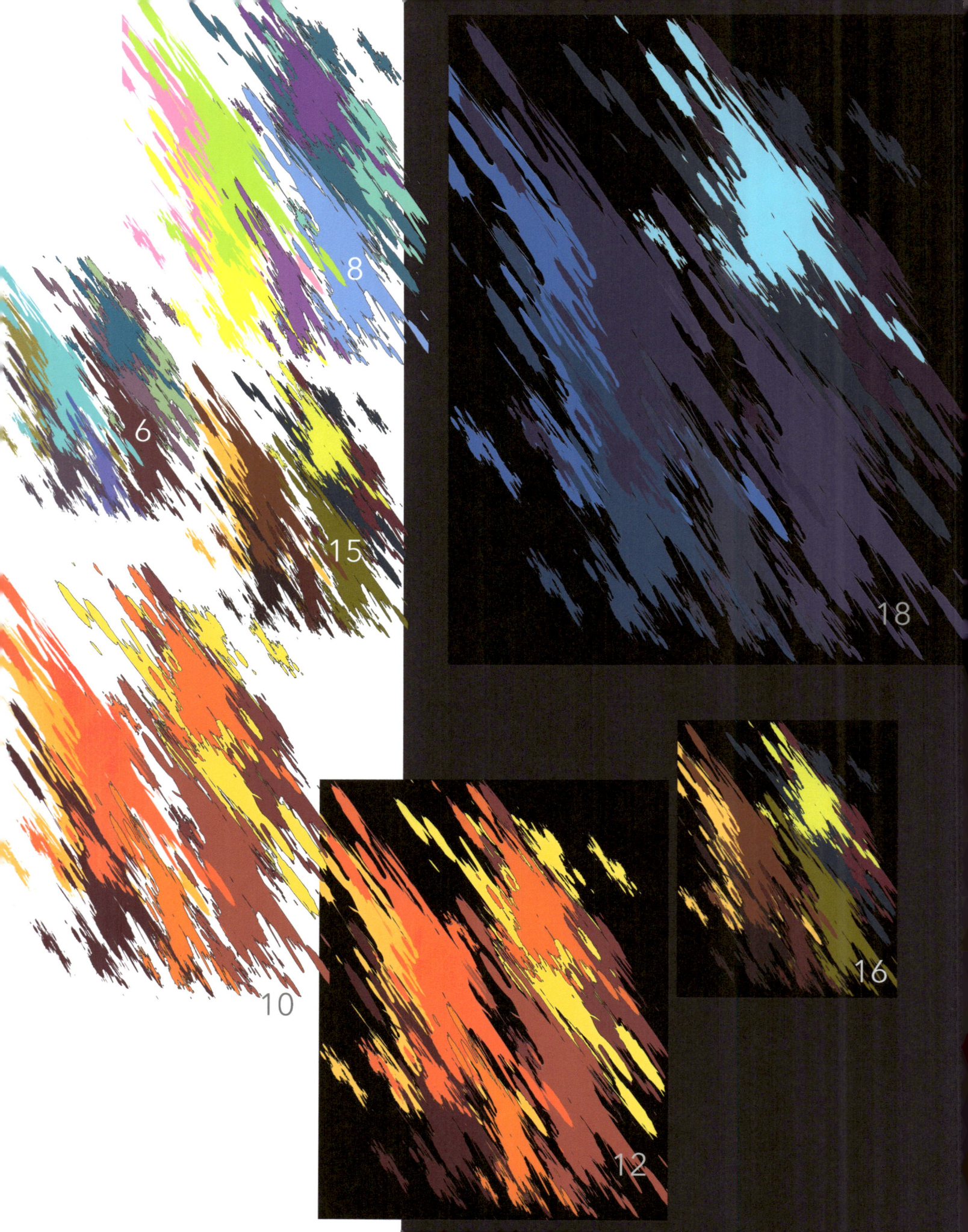

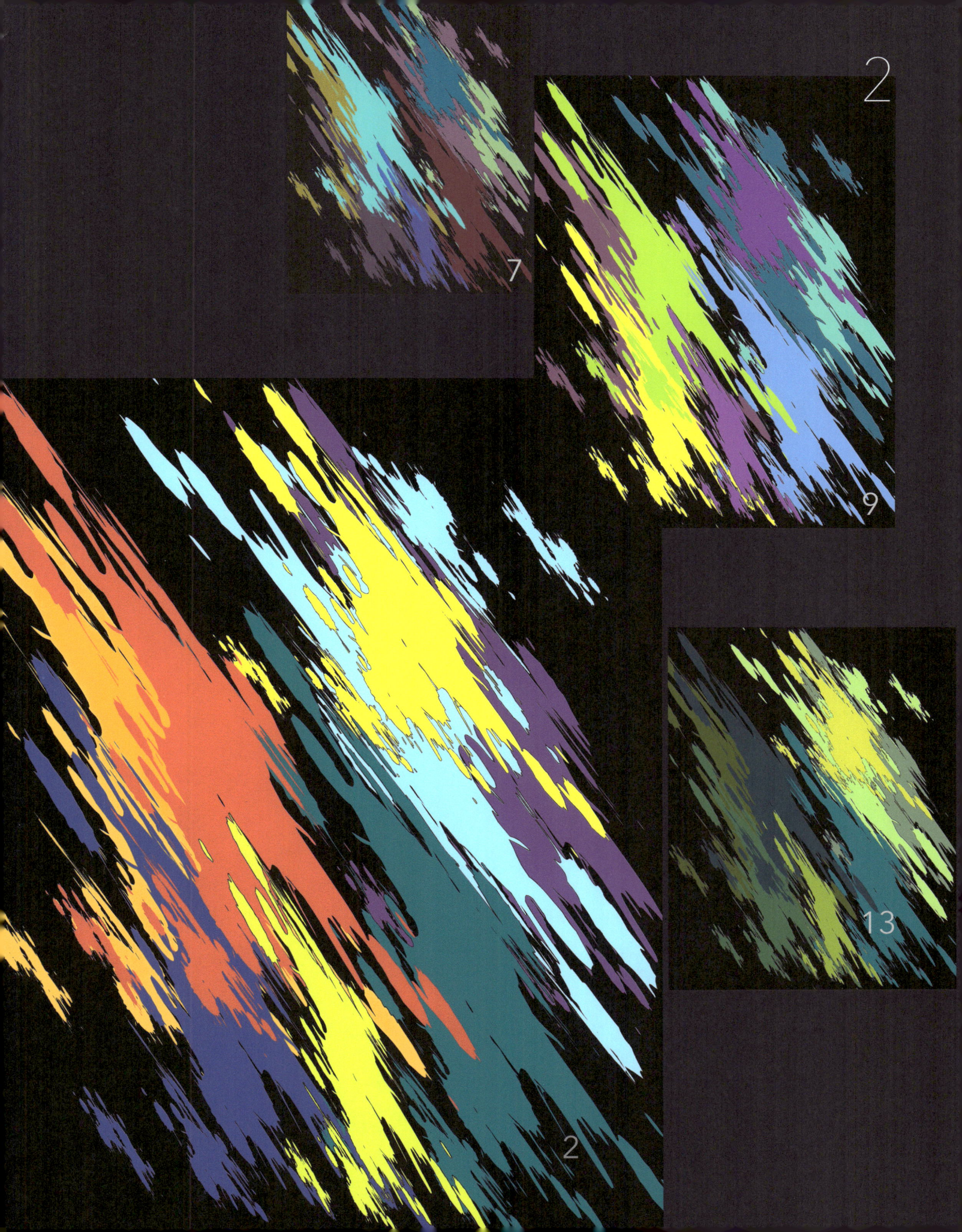

road

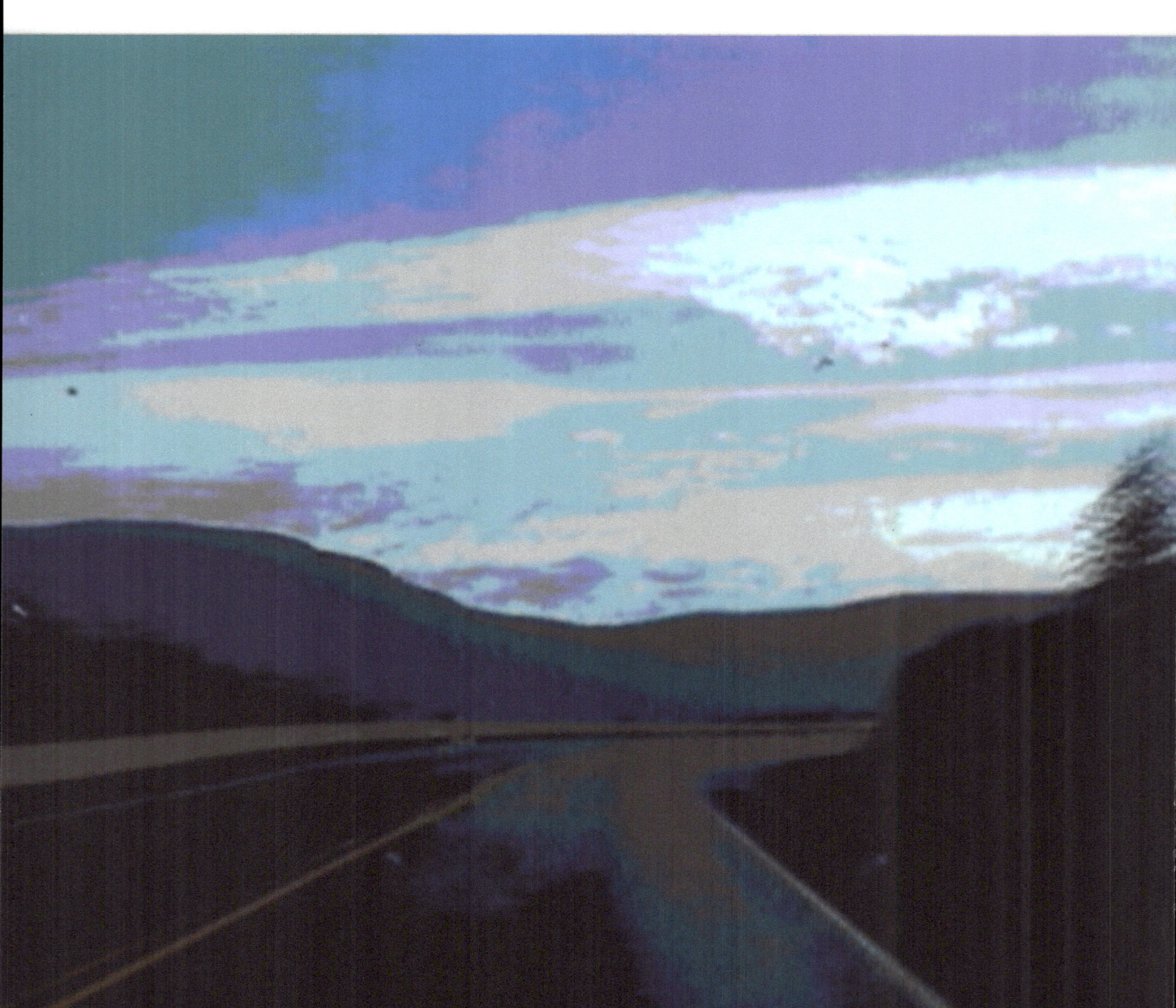

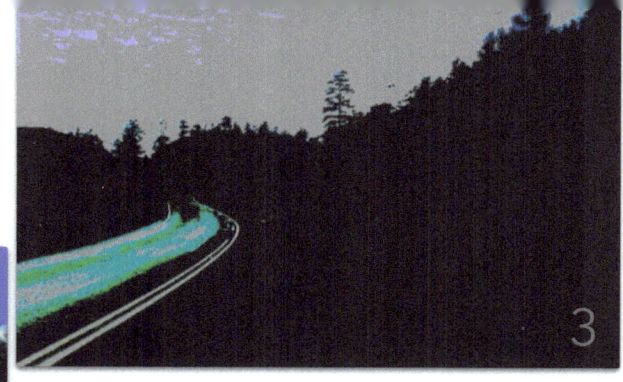

3

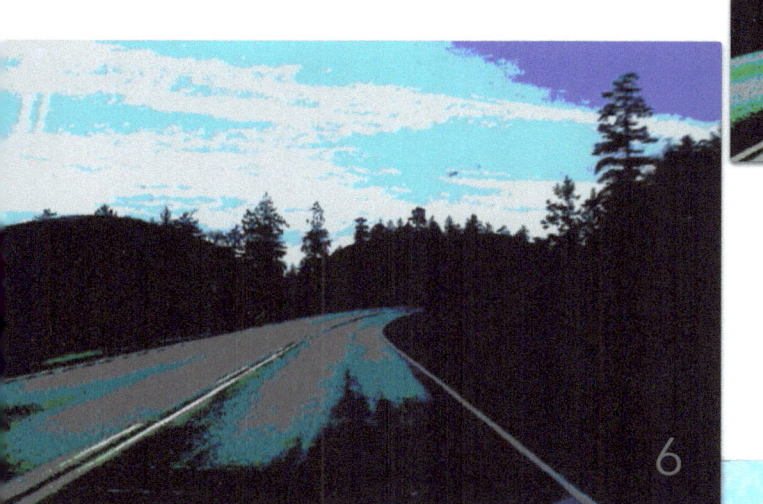

6

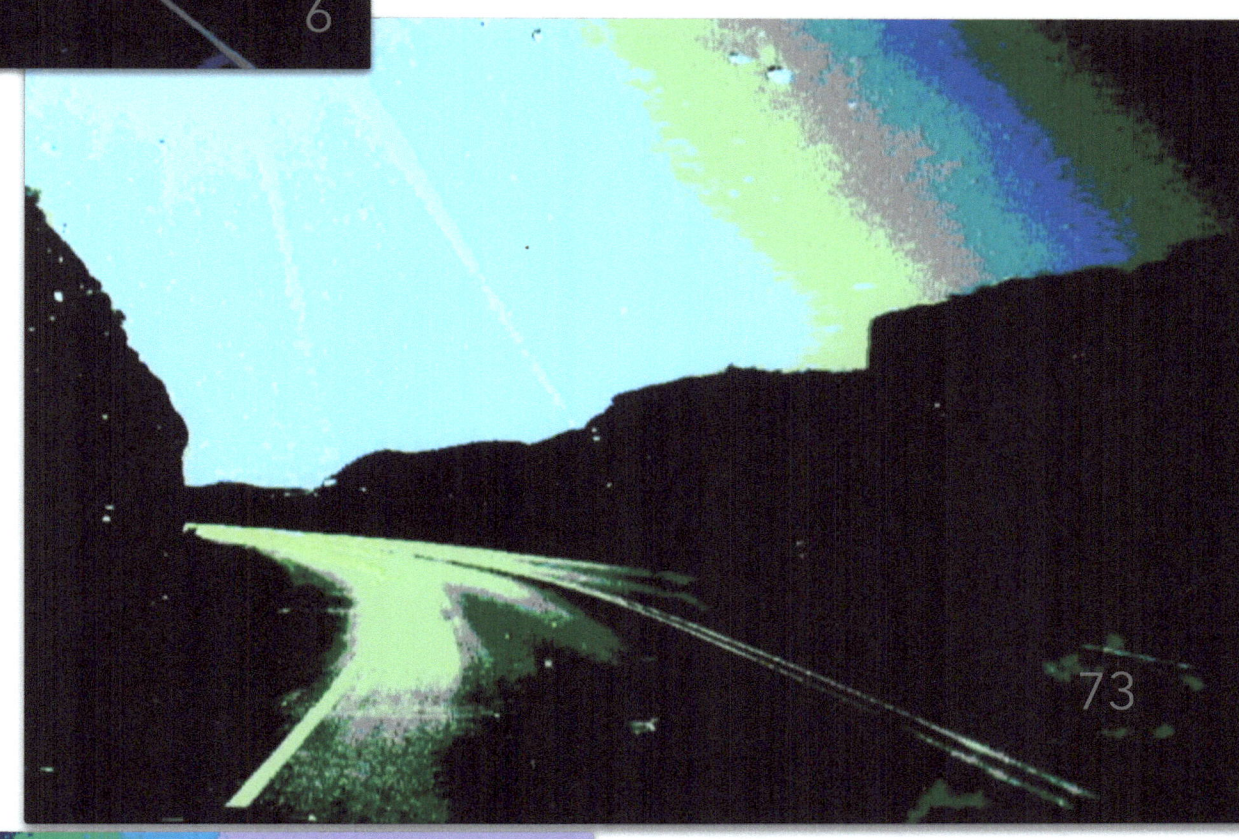

73

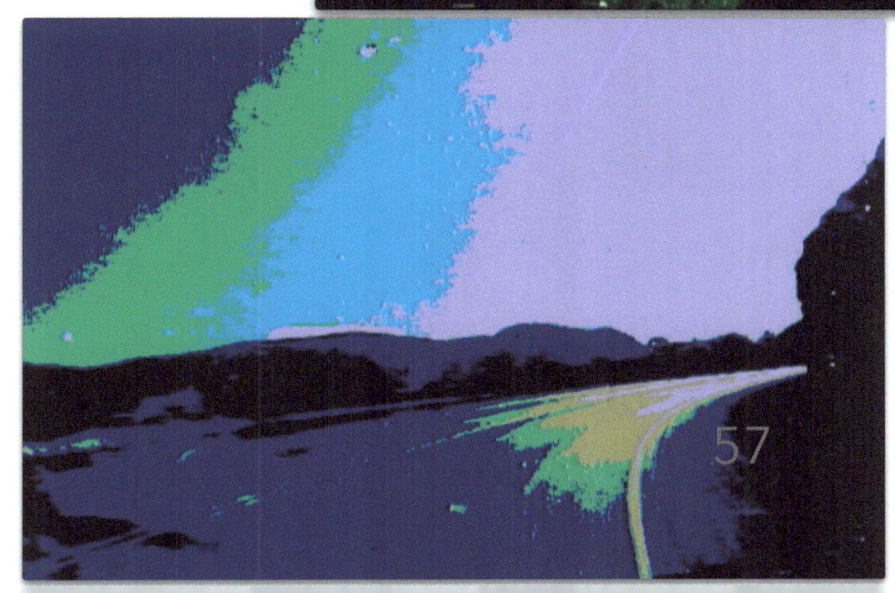

57

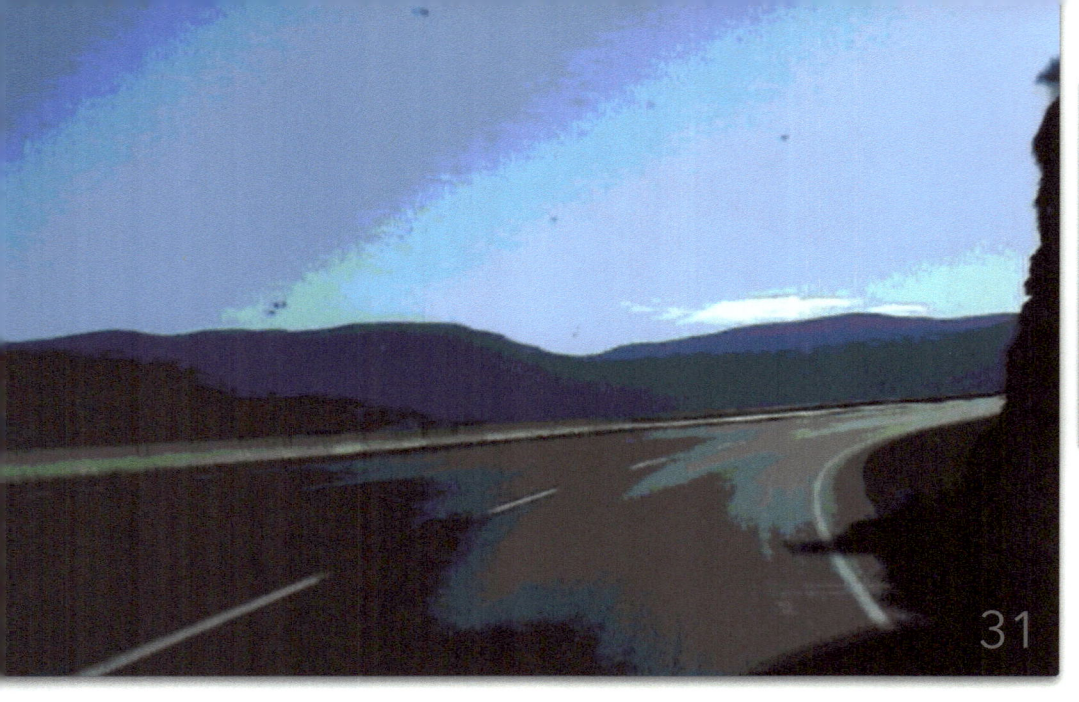

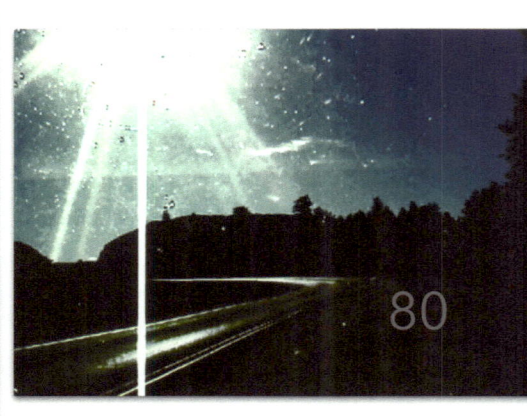

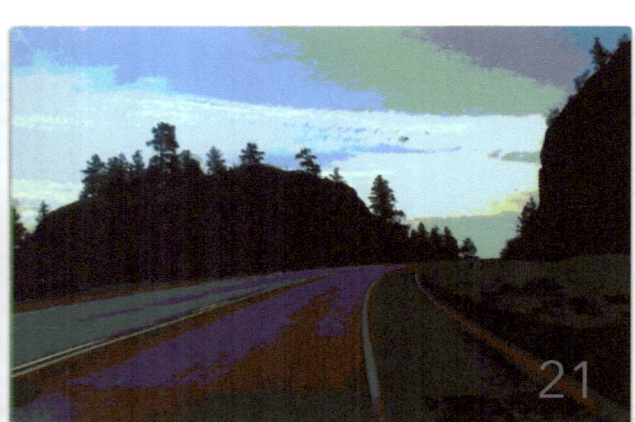

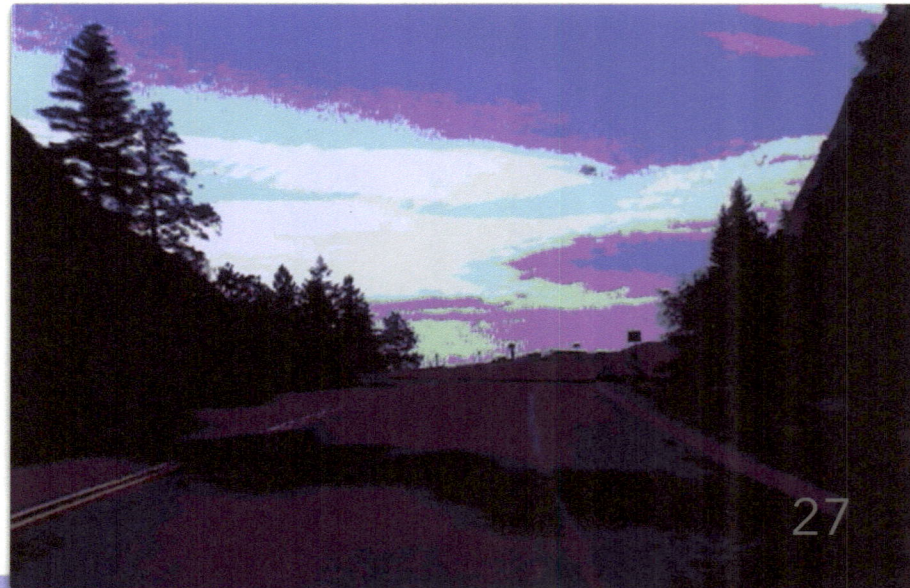

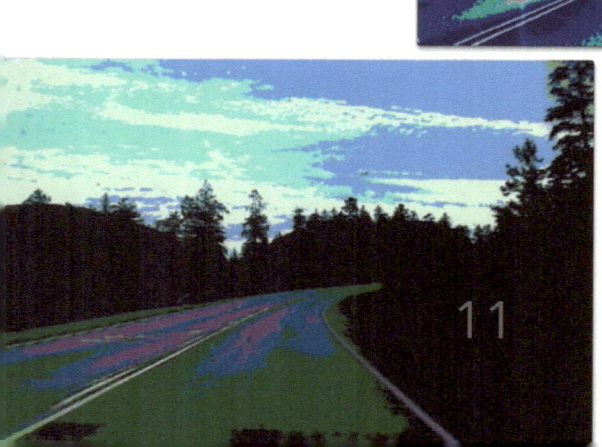

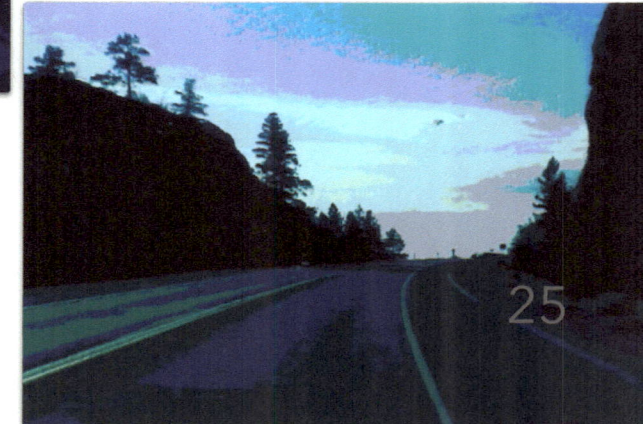

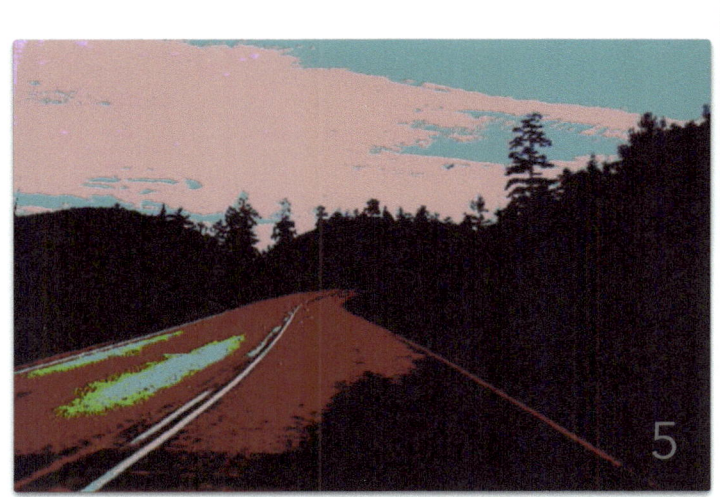

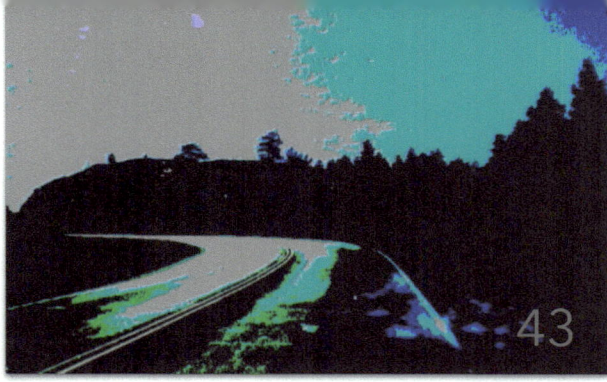

4

43

5

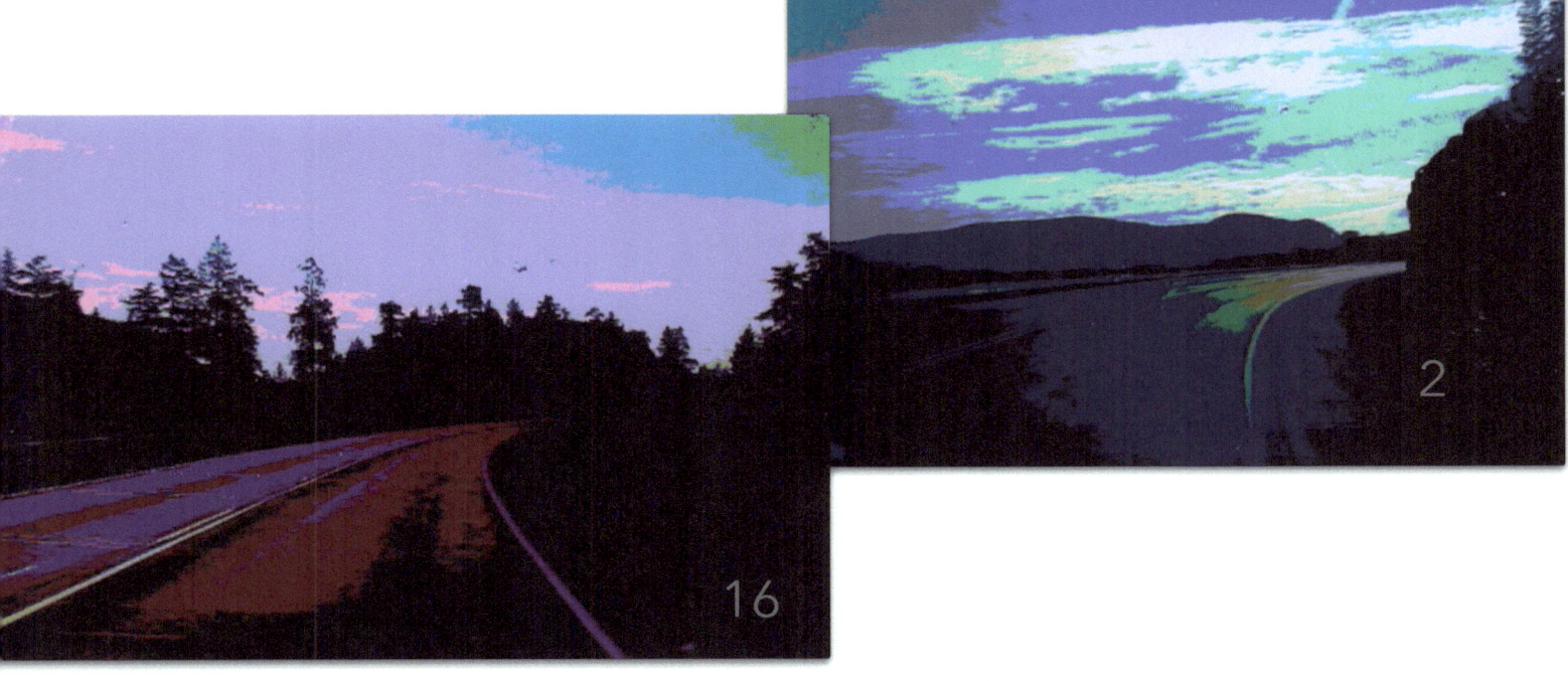

2

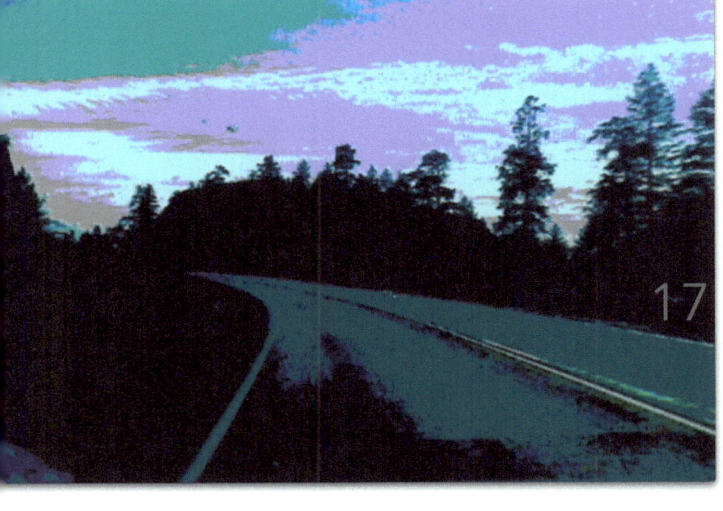

16

17

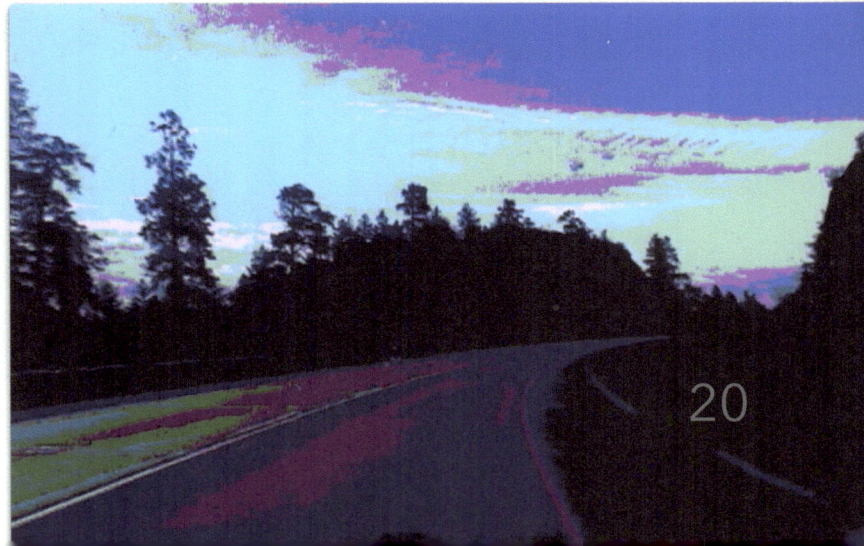

20

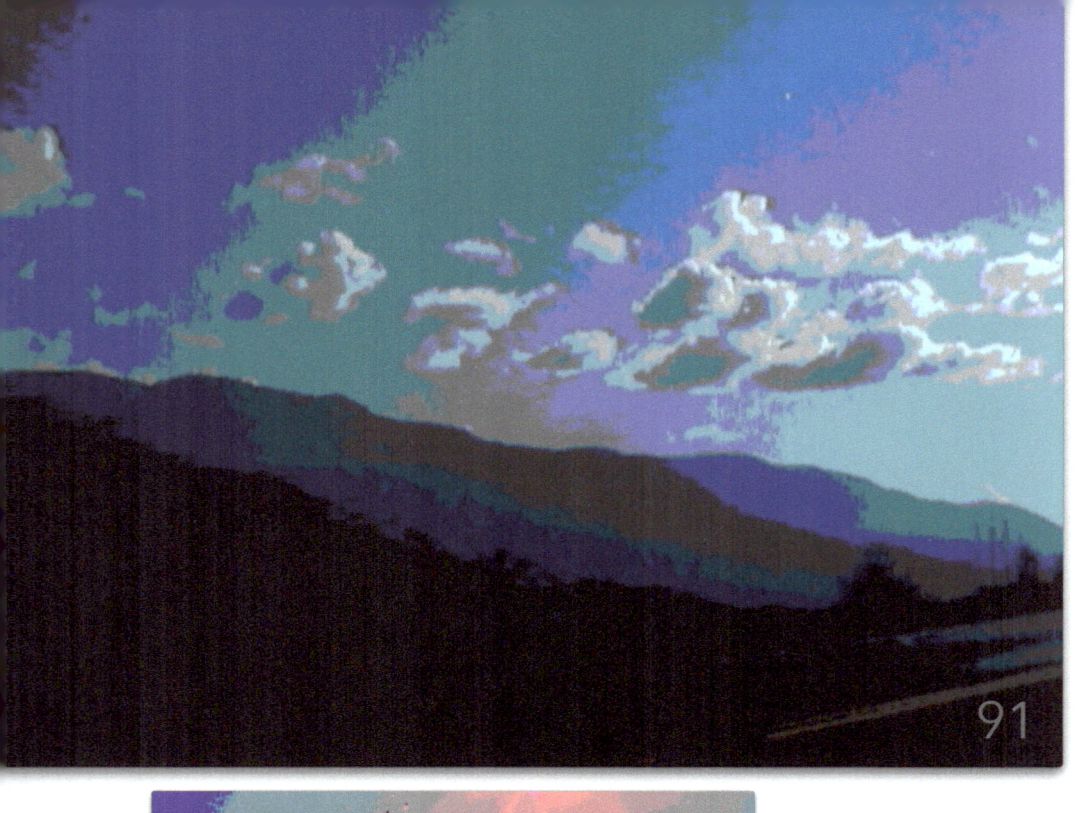

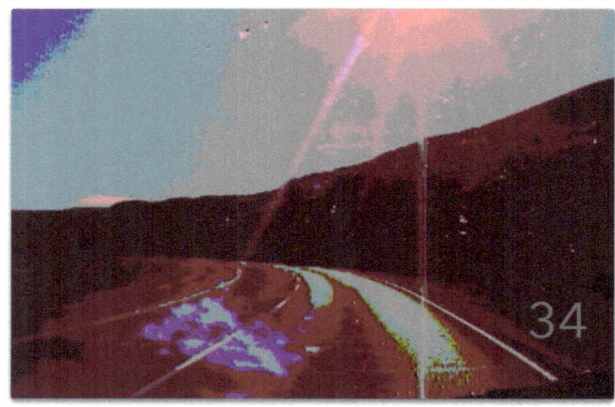

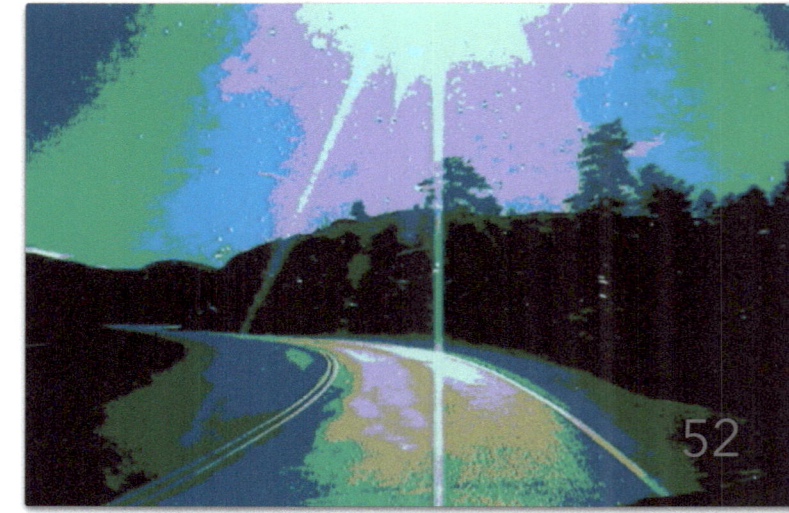

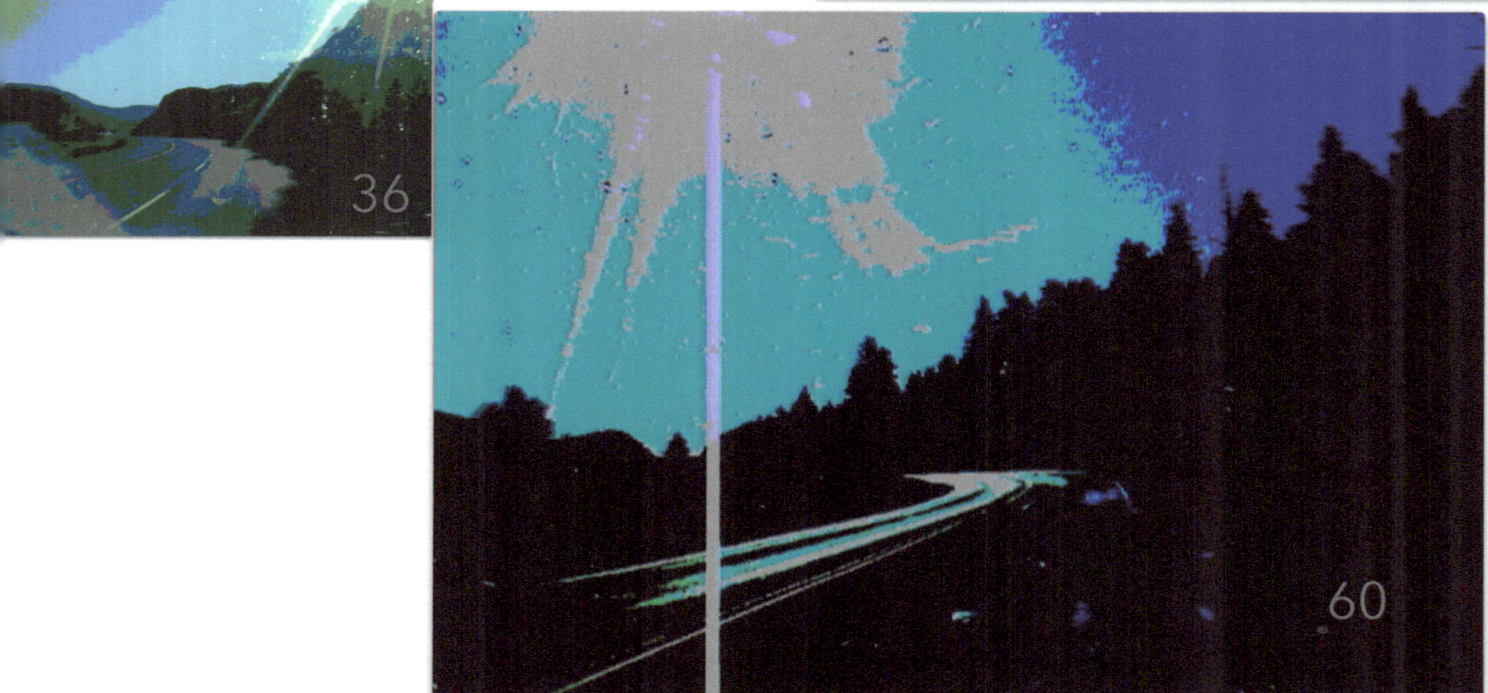

5

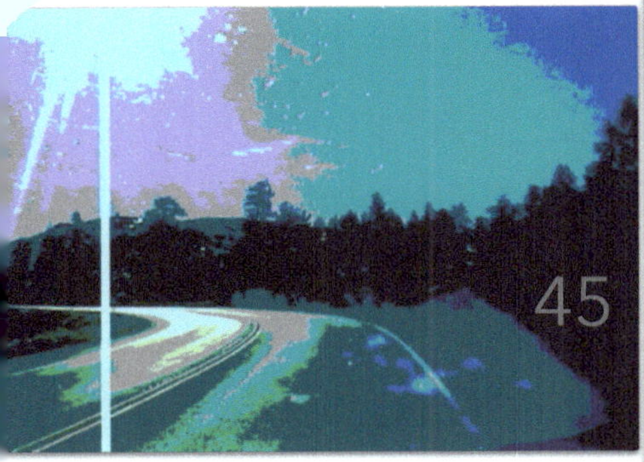

45

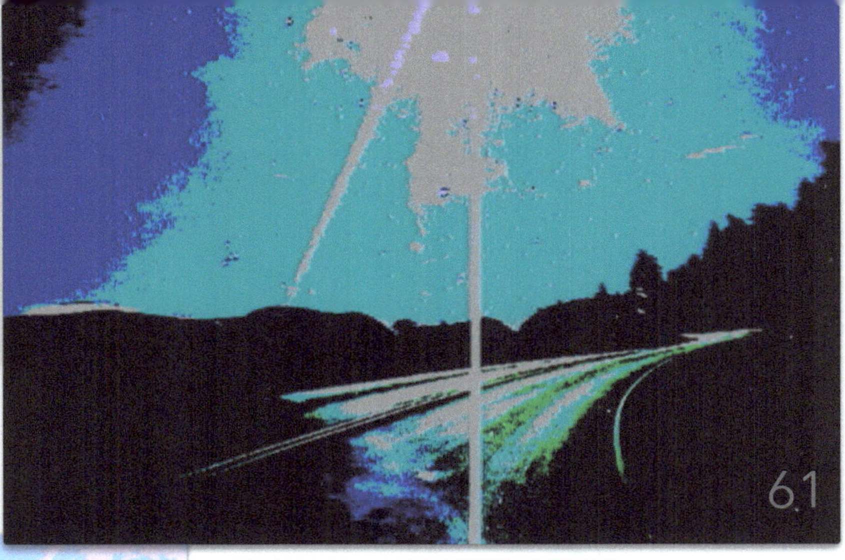

61

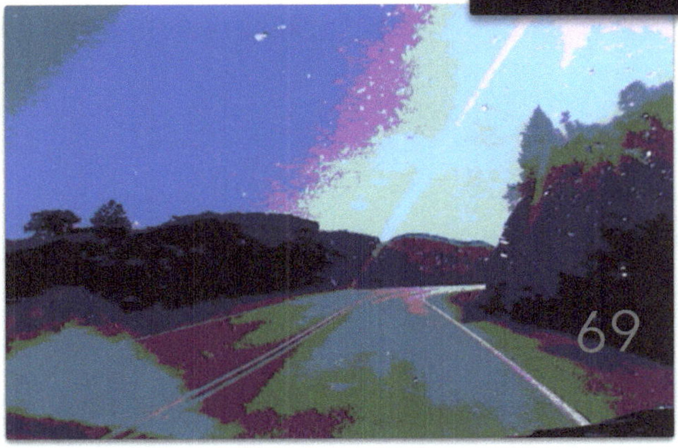

69

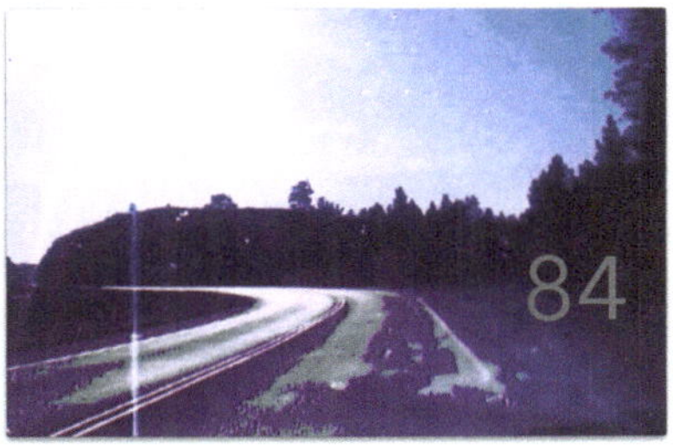

84

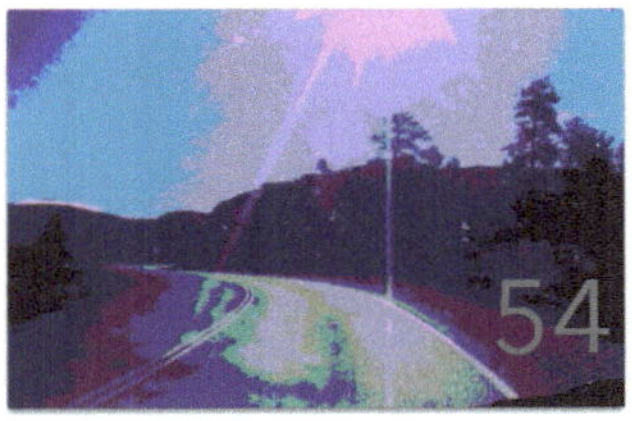

54

Trans-Canada B.C.

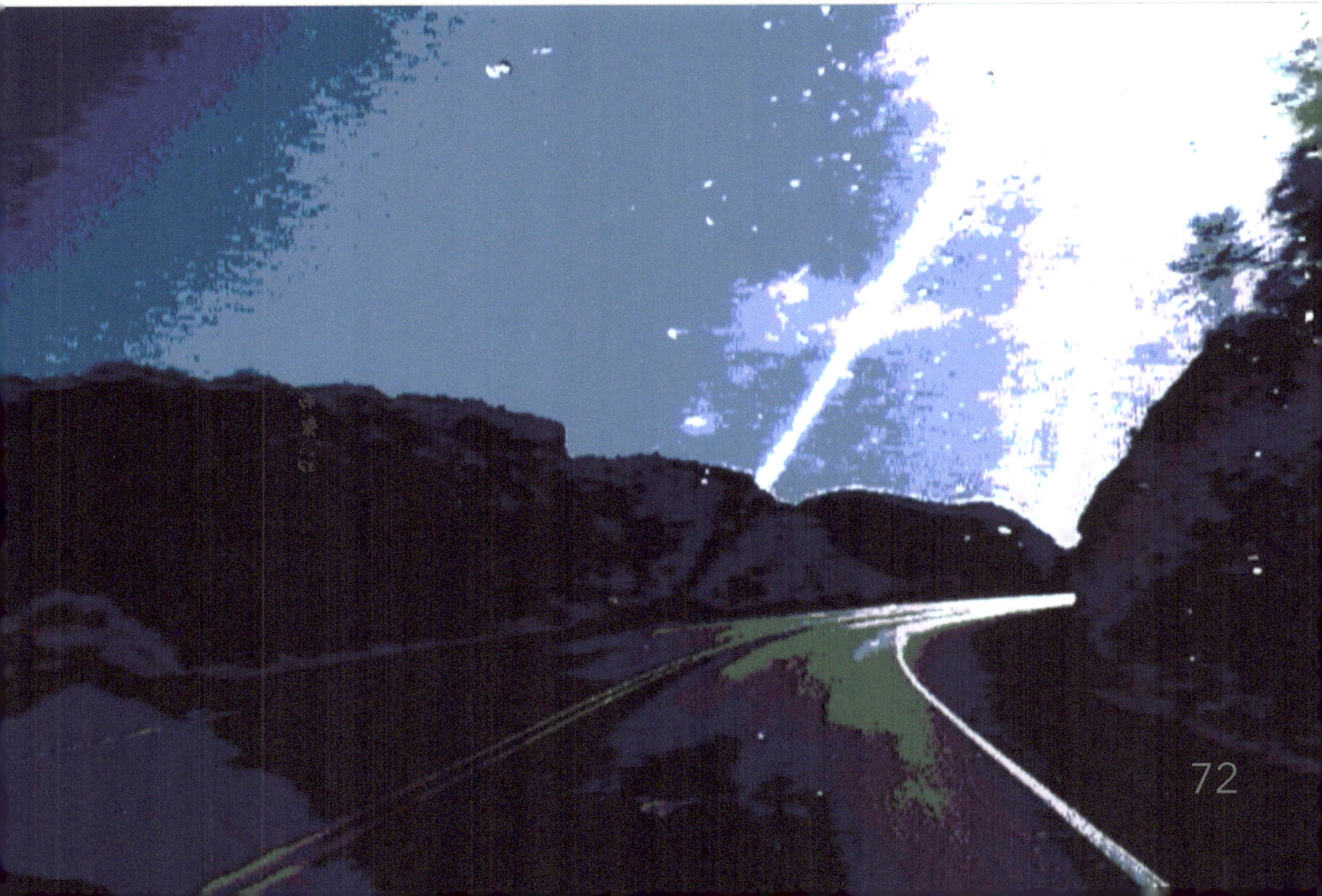

72

transition

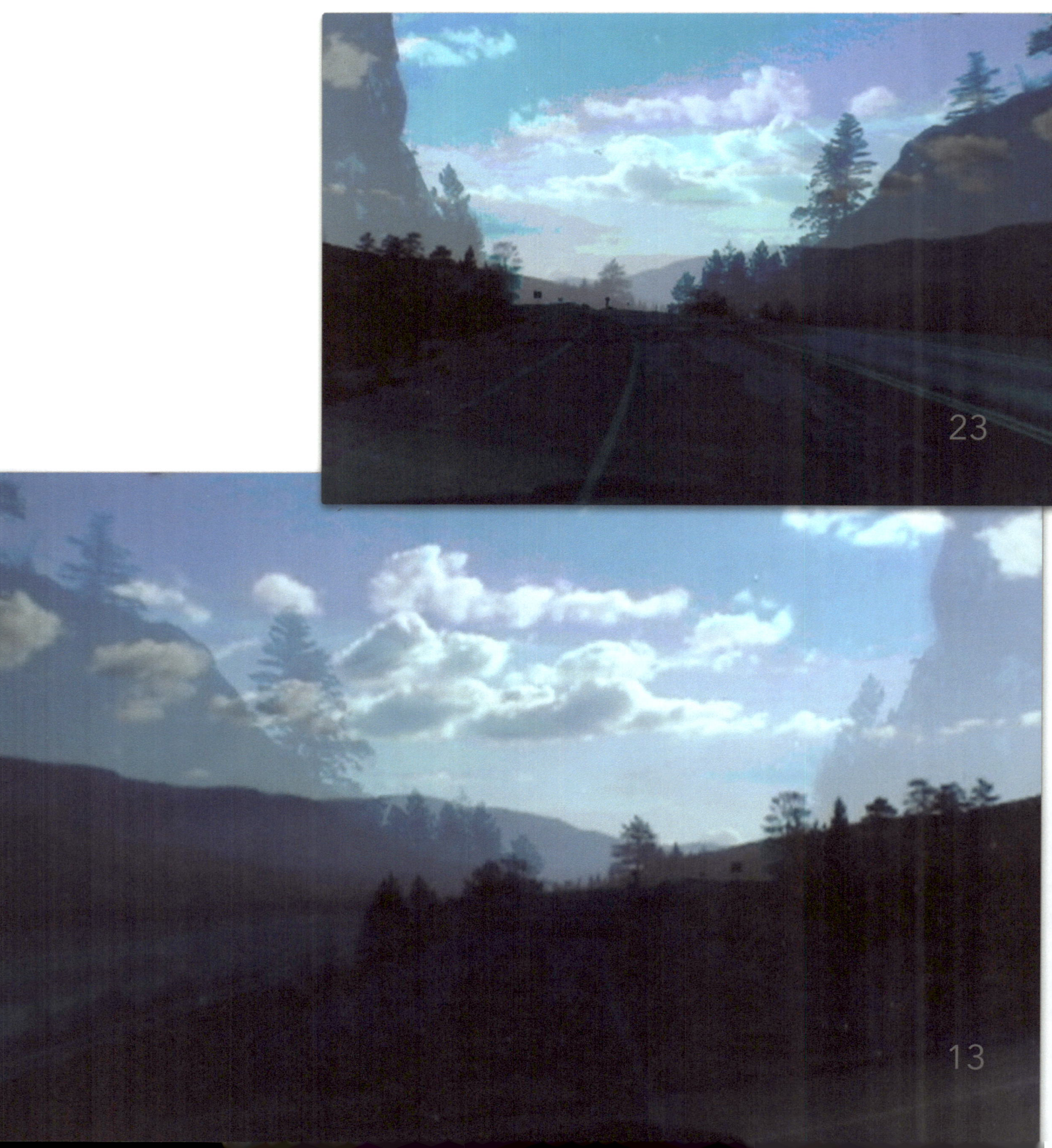

23

13

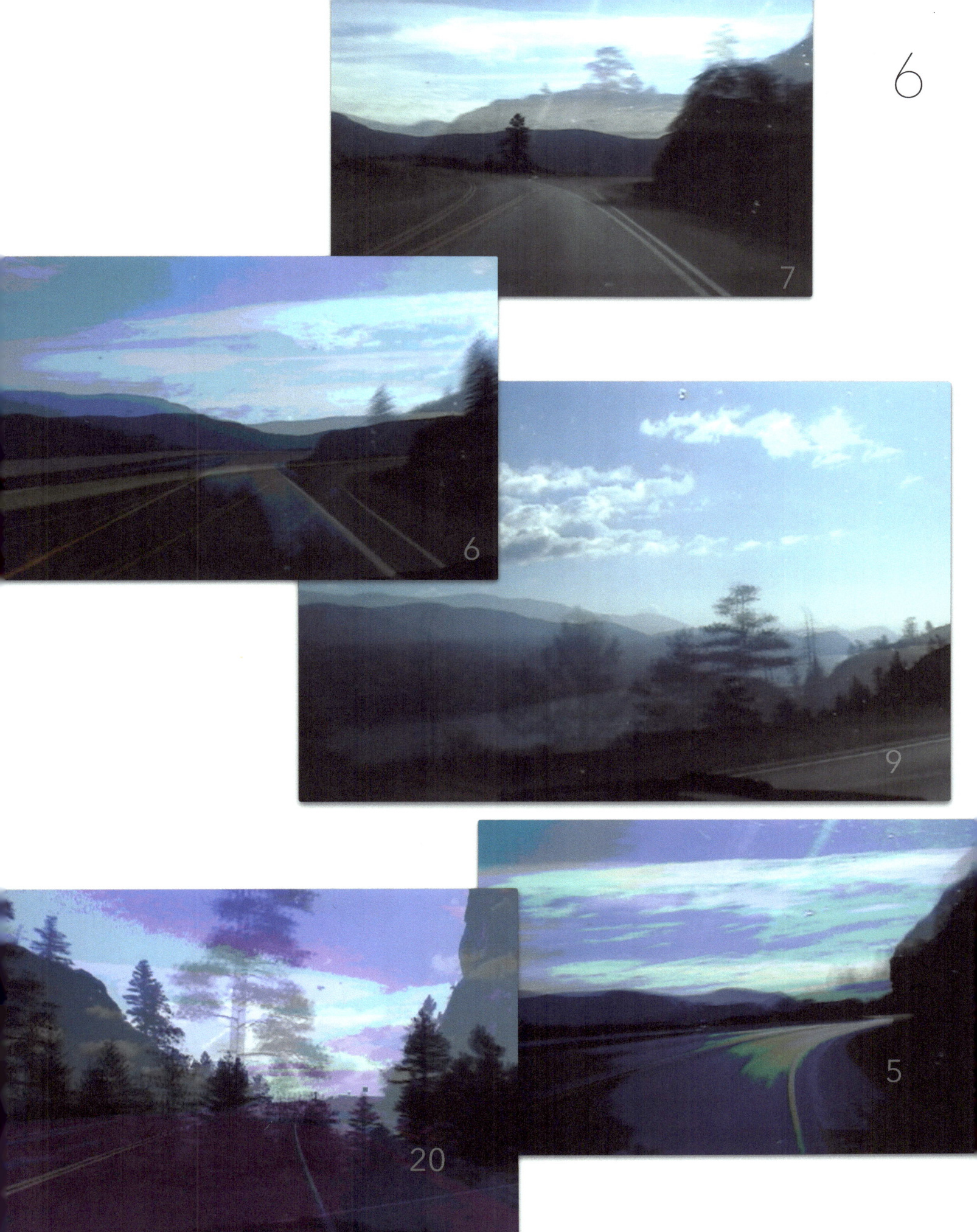

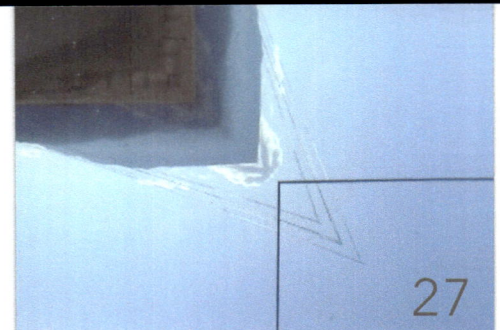

reflection

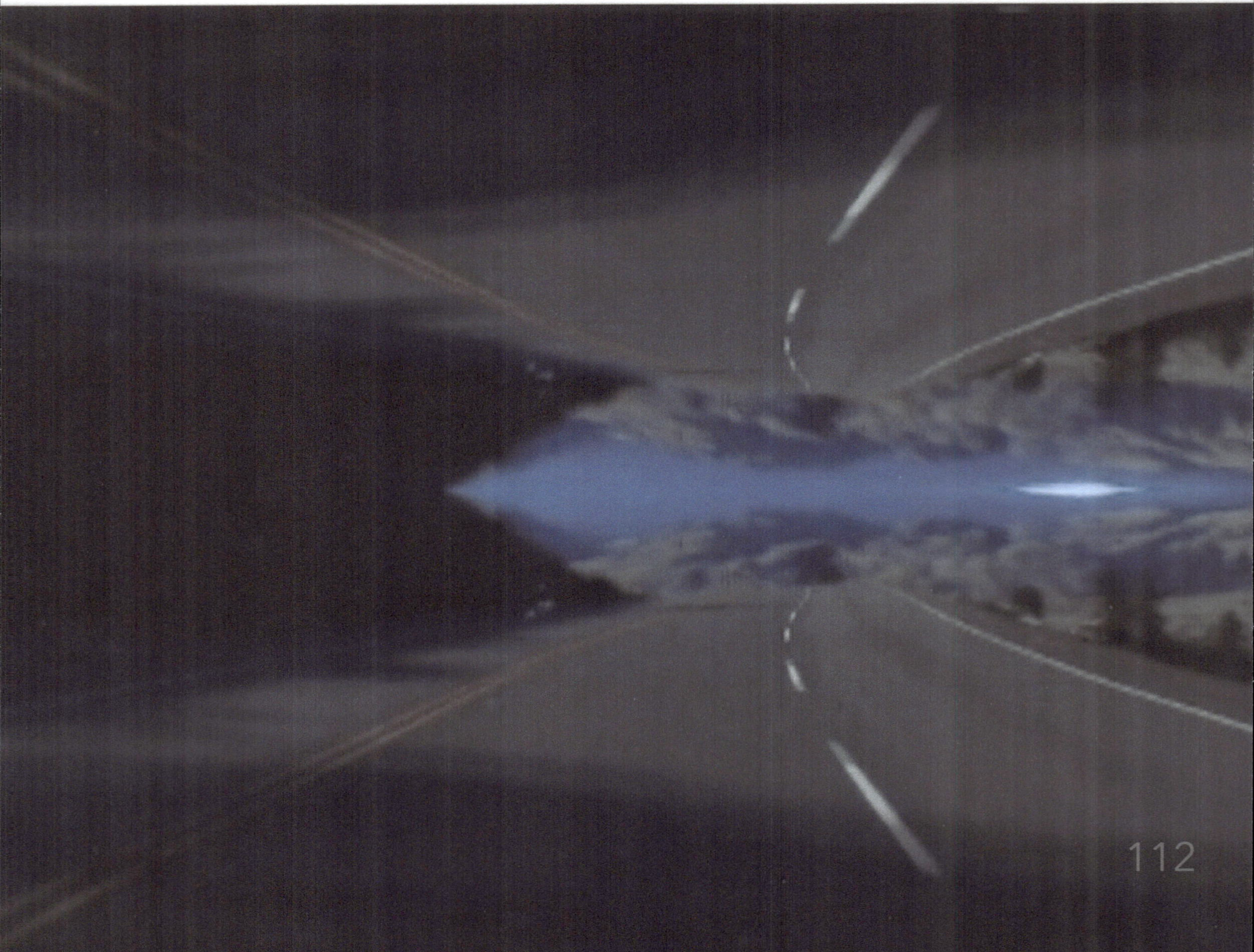

7

134

34

24

46

42

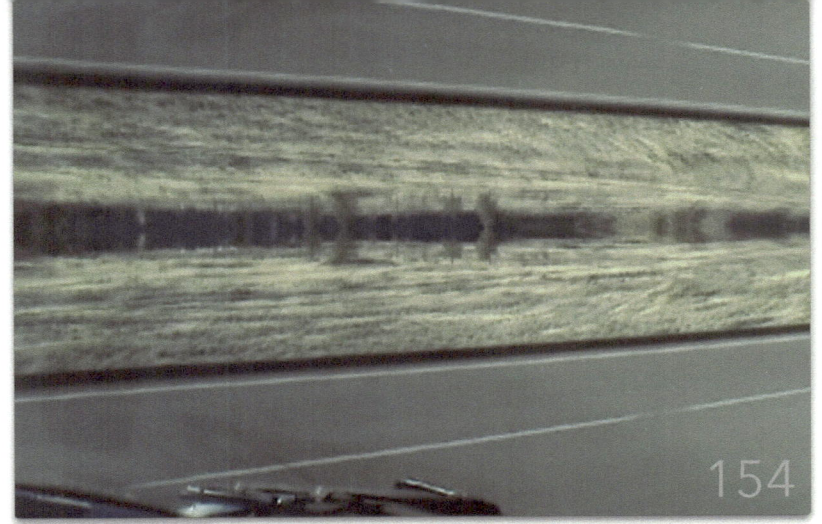

154

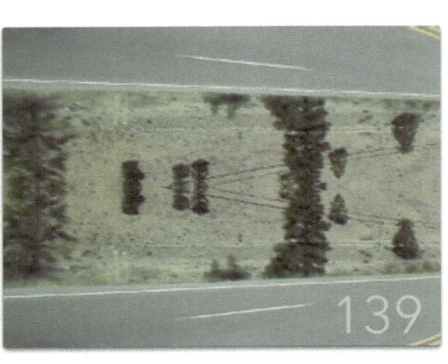

139

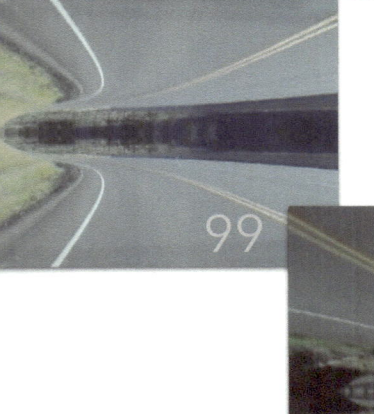

99

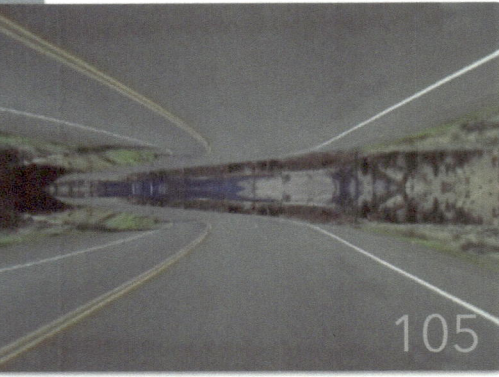

105

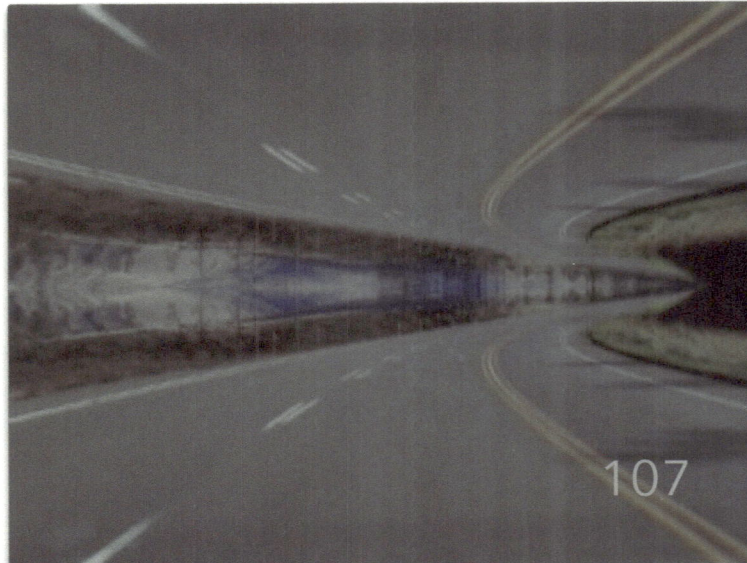

107

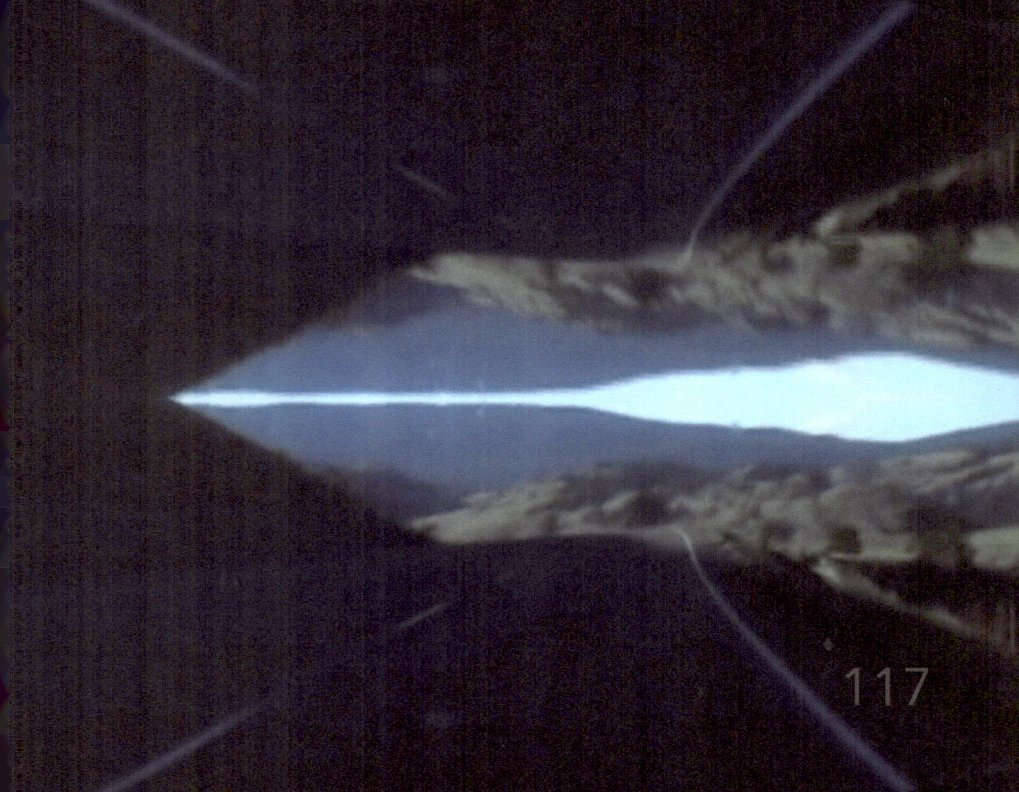

117

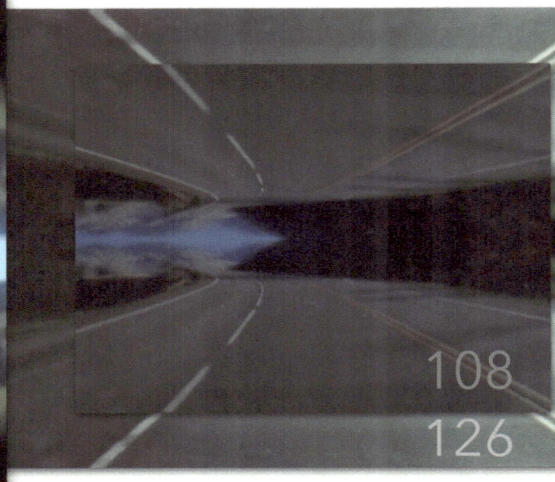

108

126

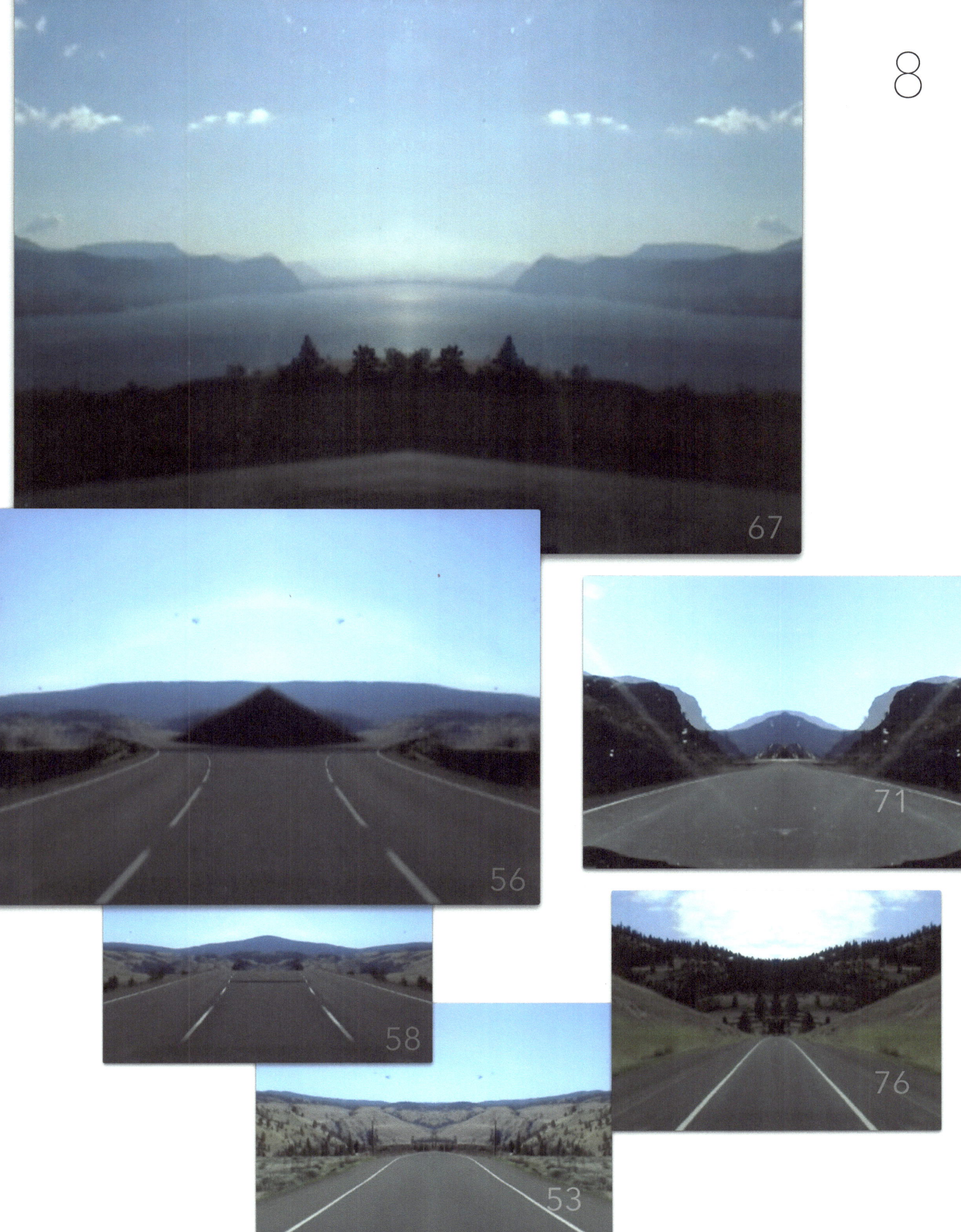

illusion

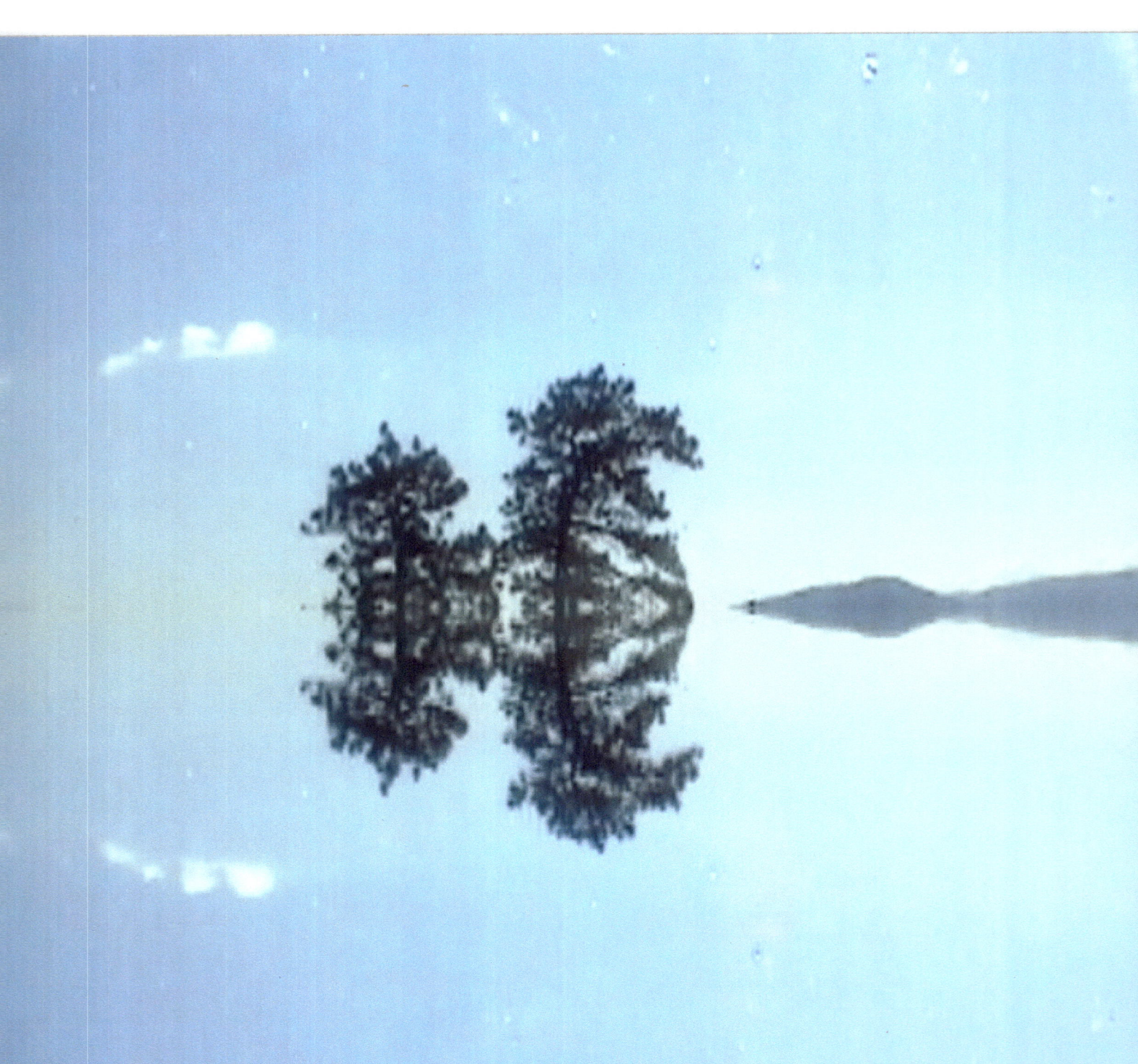

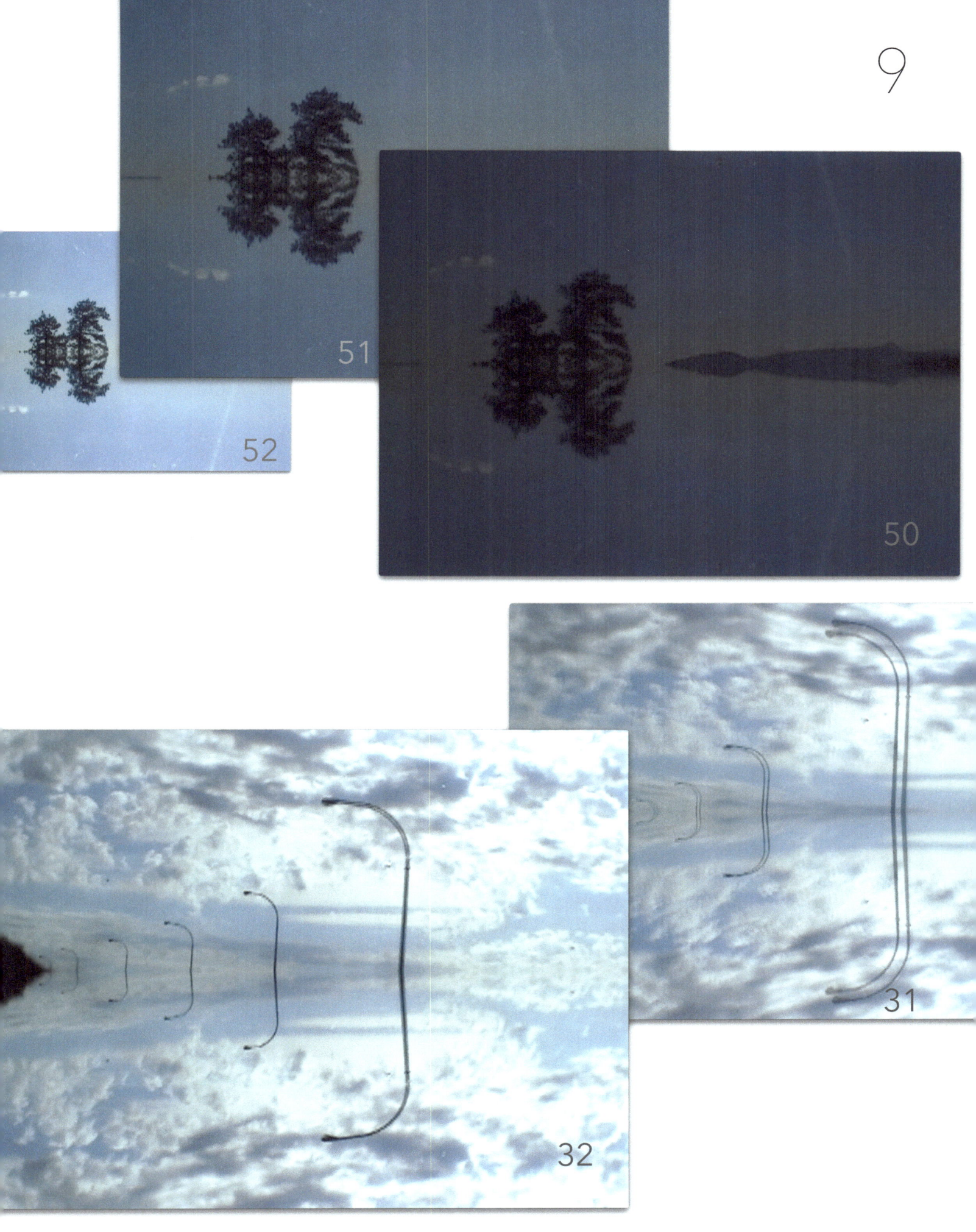

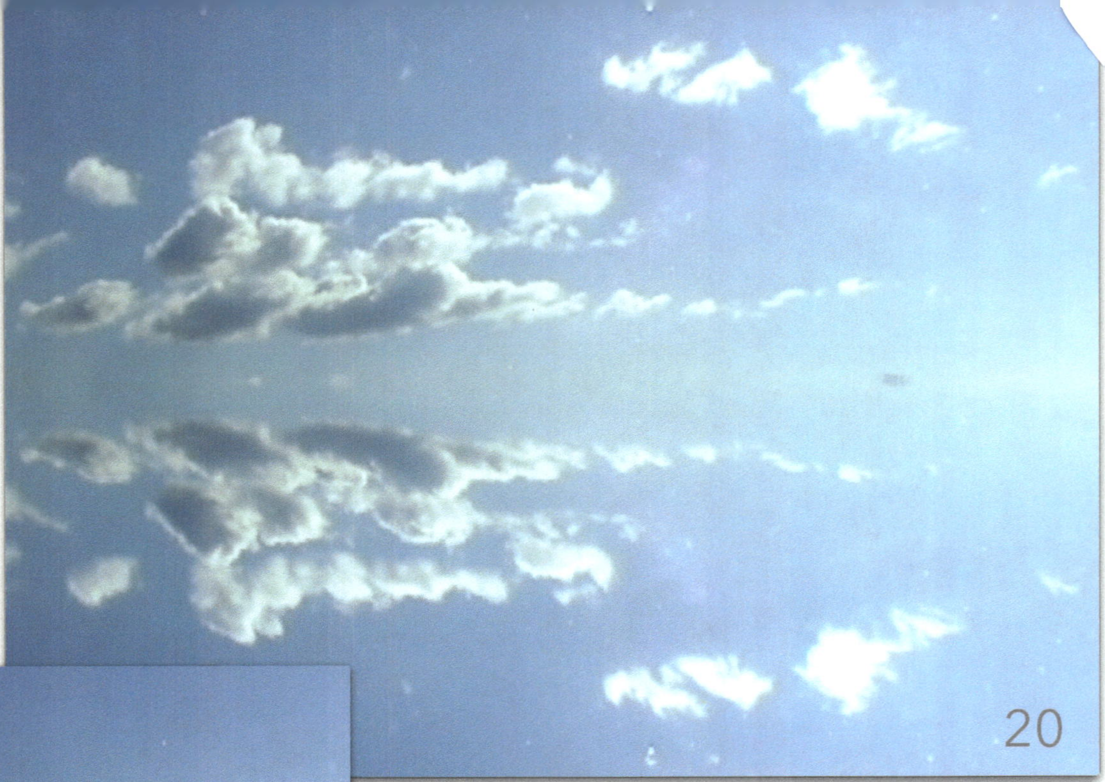

20

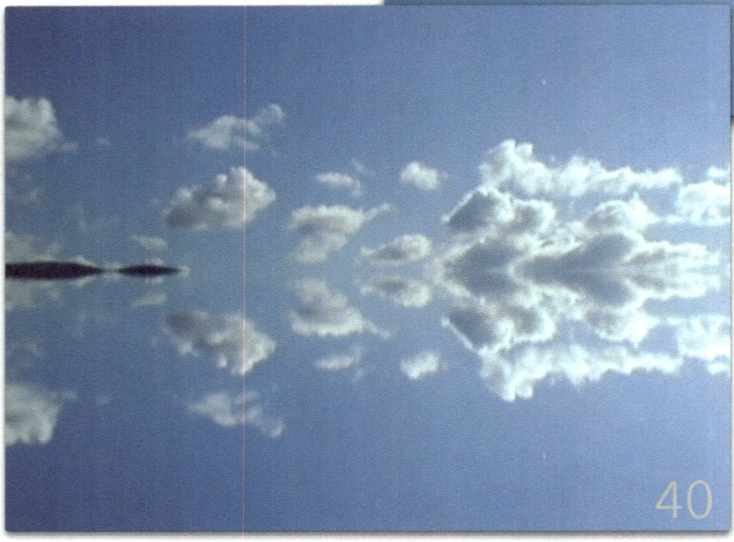

40

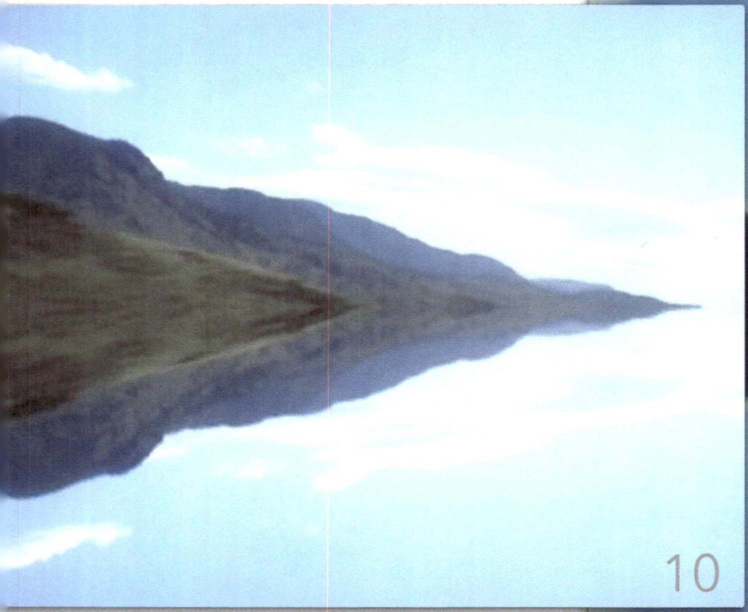

10

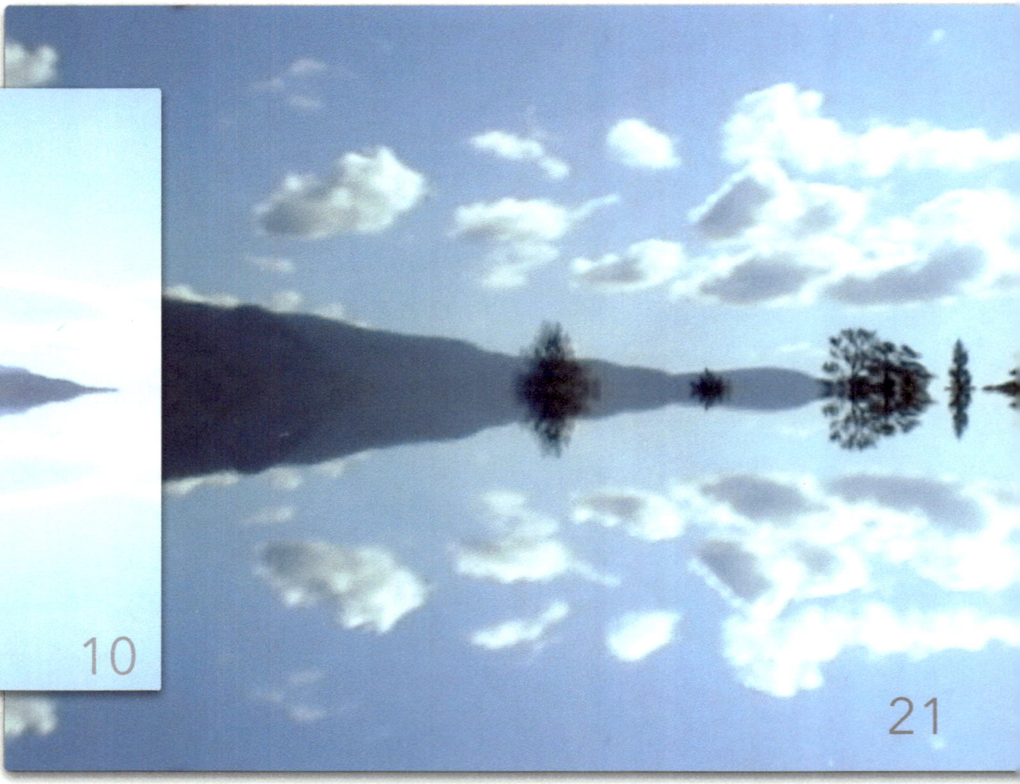

21

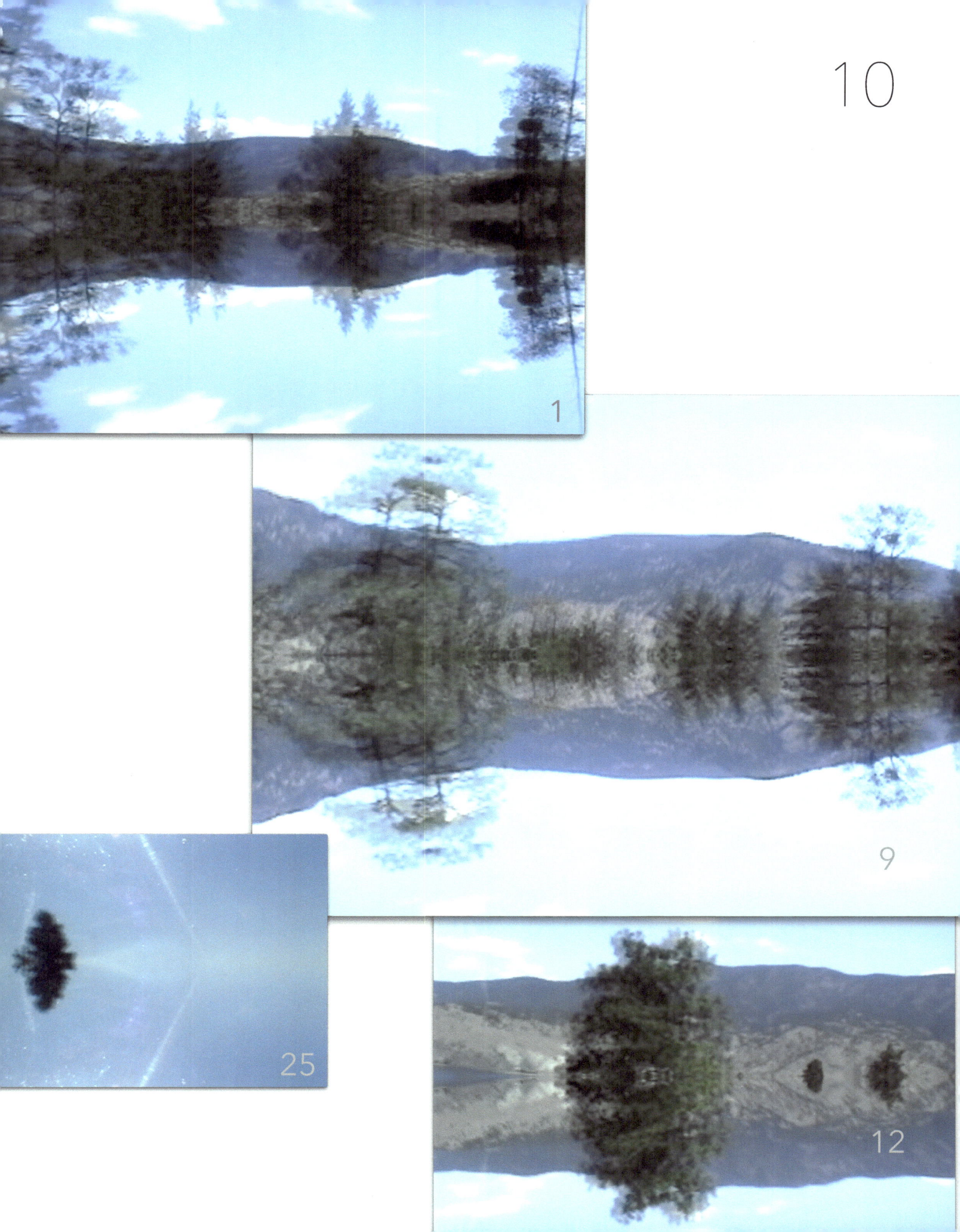

fire

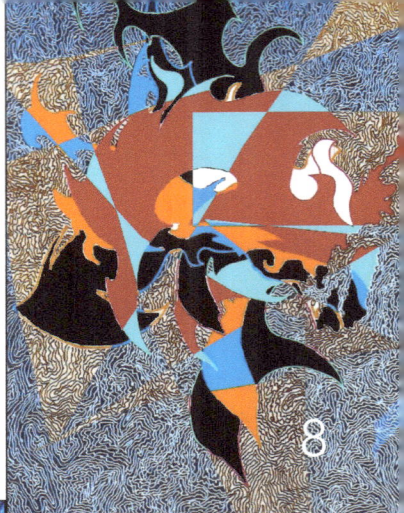

8

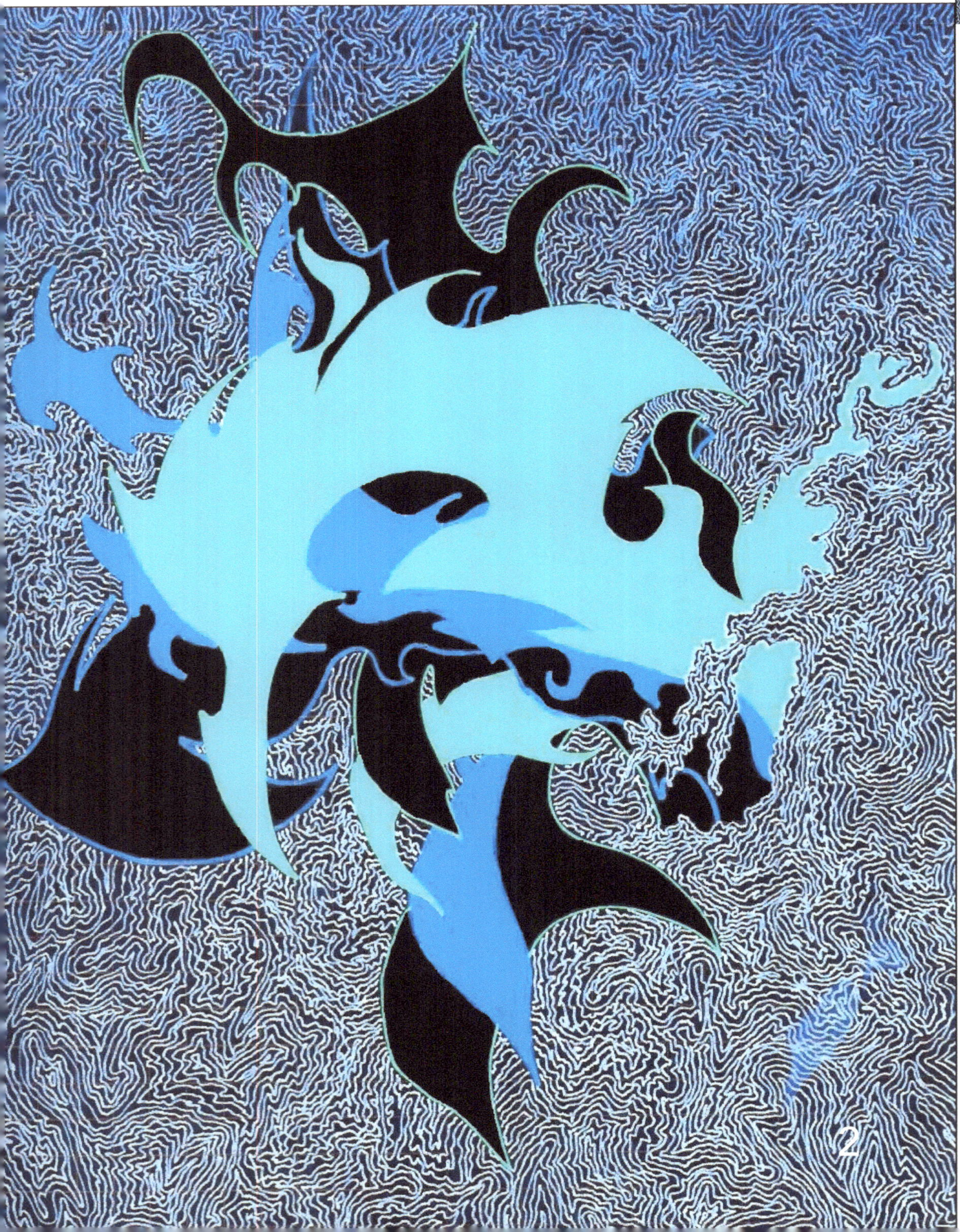

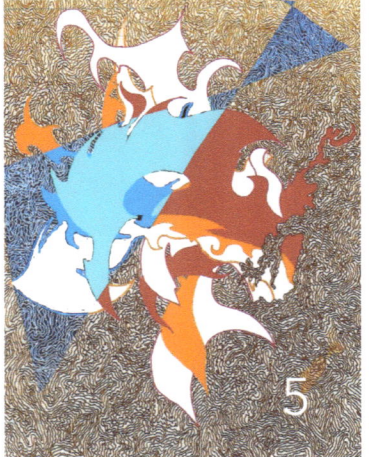

5

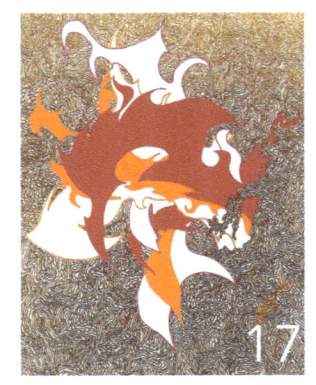

17

2

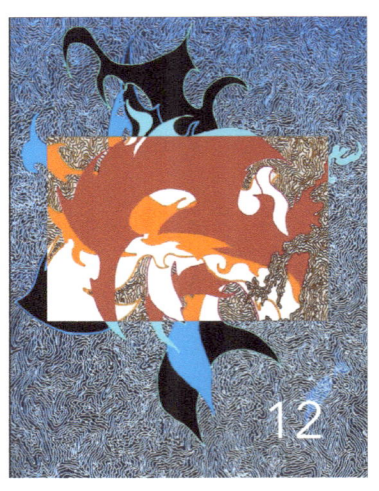

12

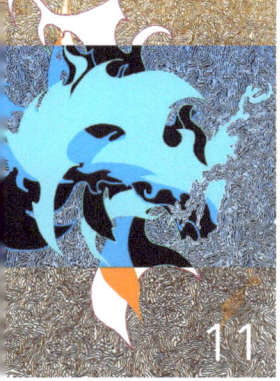

11

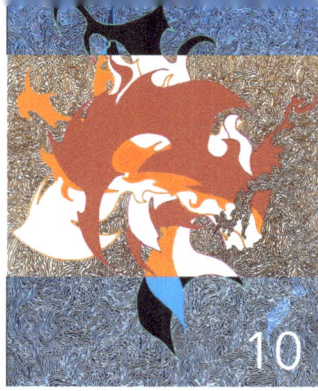

10

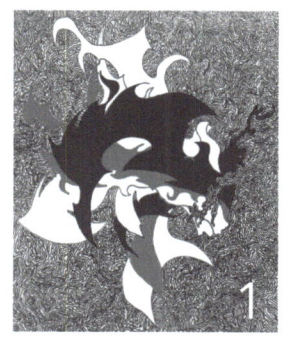

1

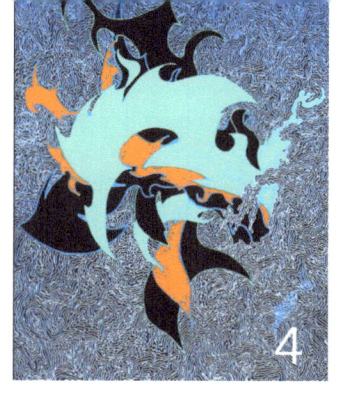

4

11

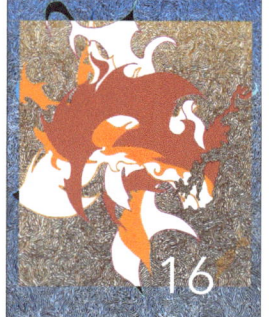

16

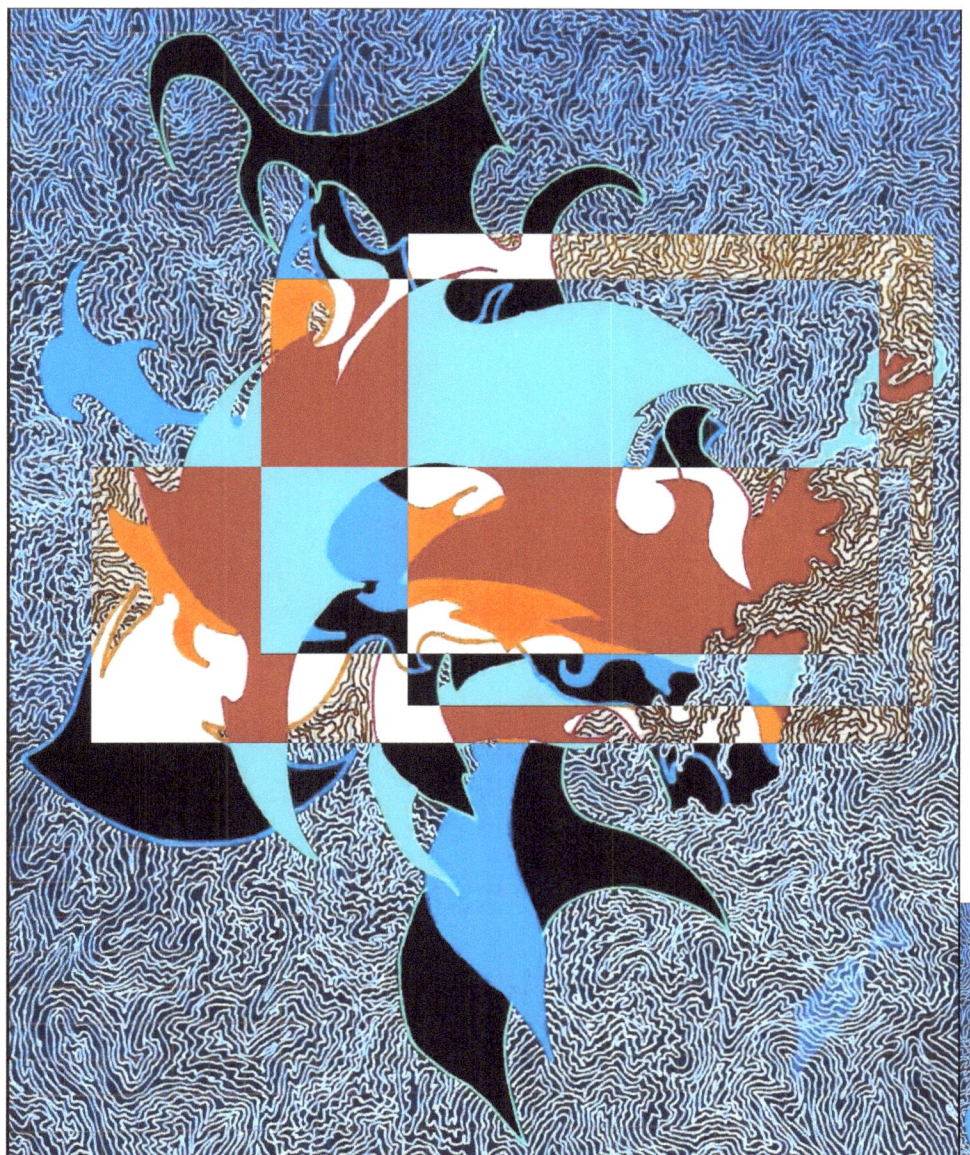

14

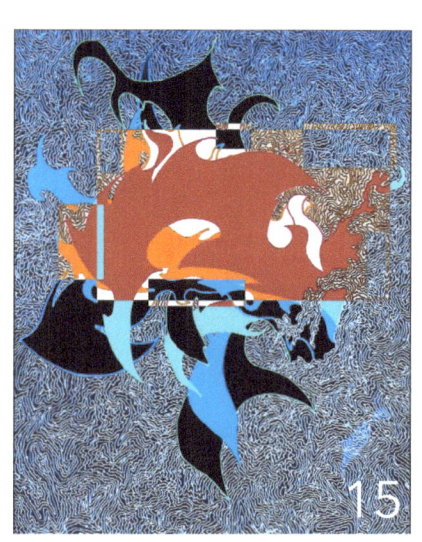

15

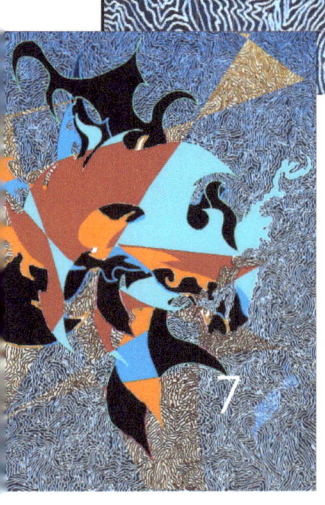

7

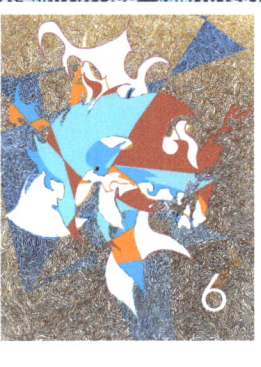

6

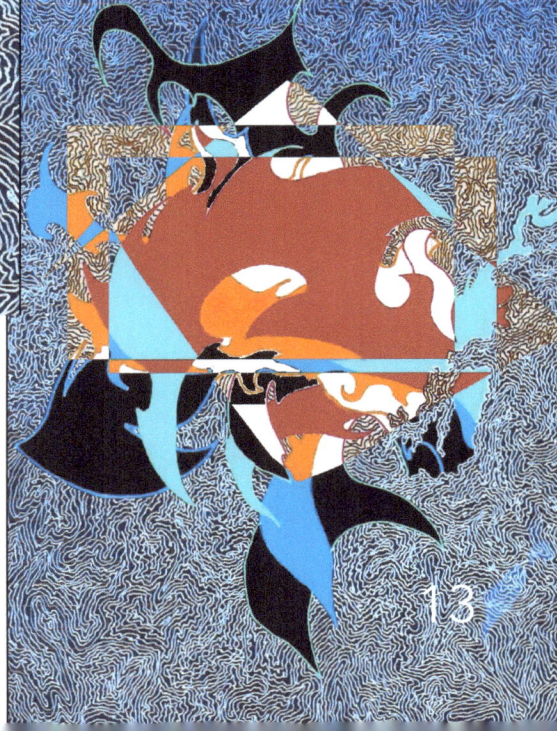

13

kaleidoscope

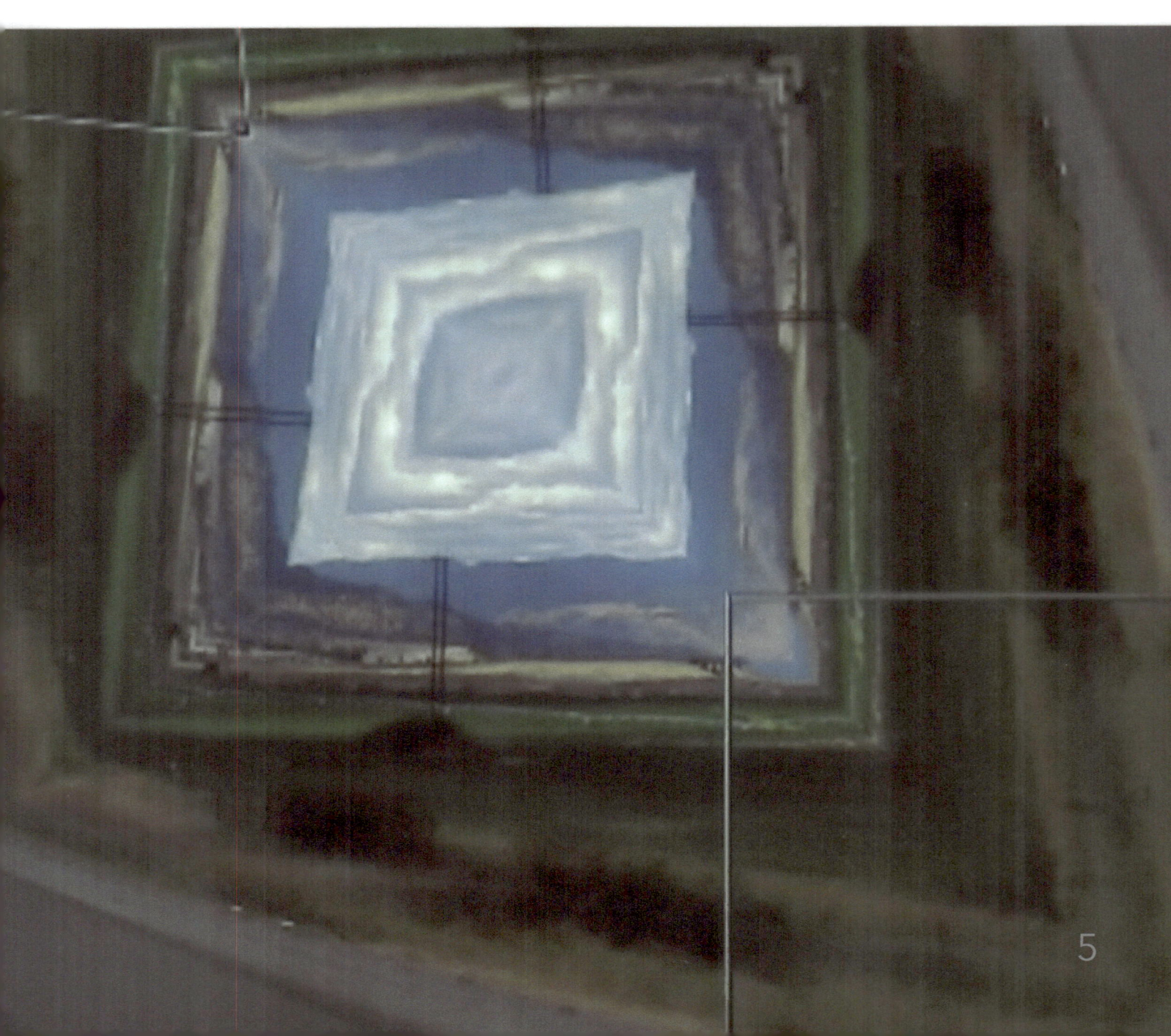

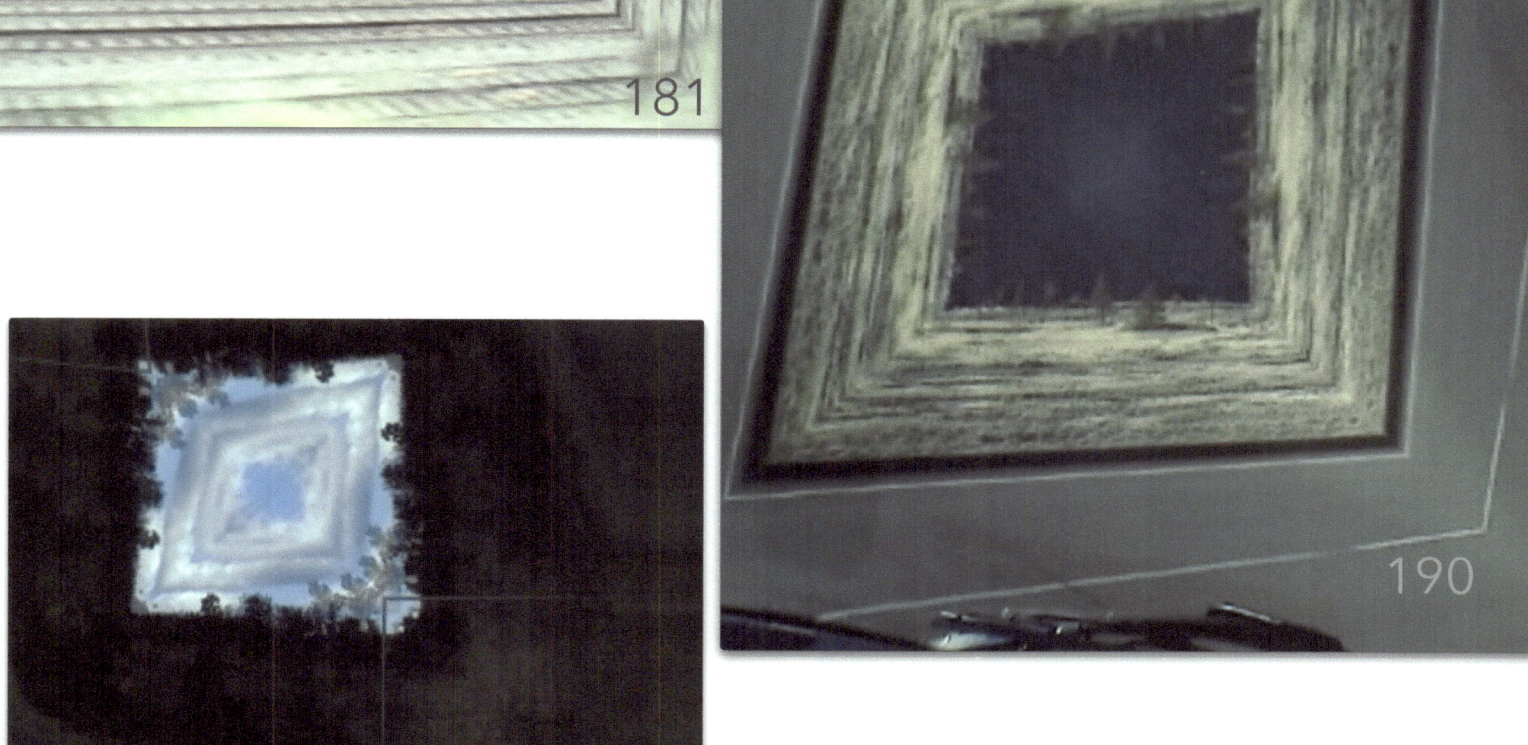

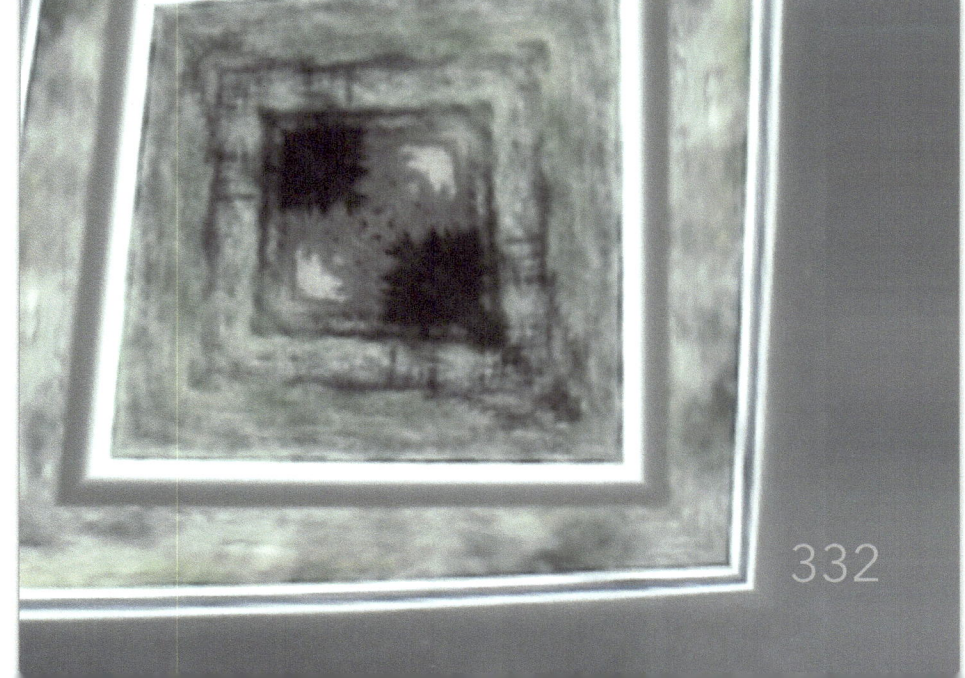

12

181

190

90

332

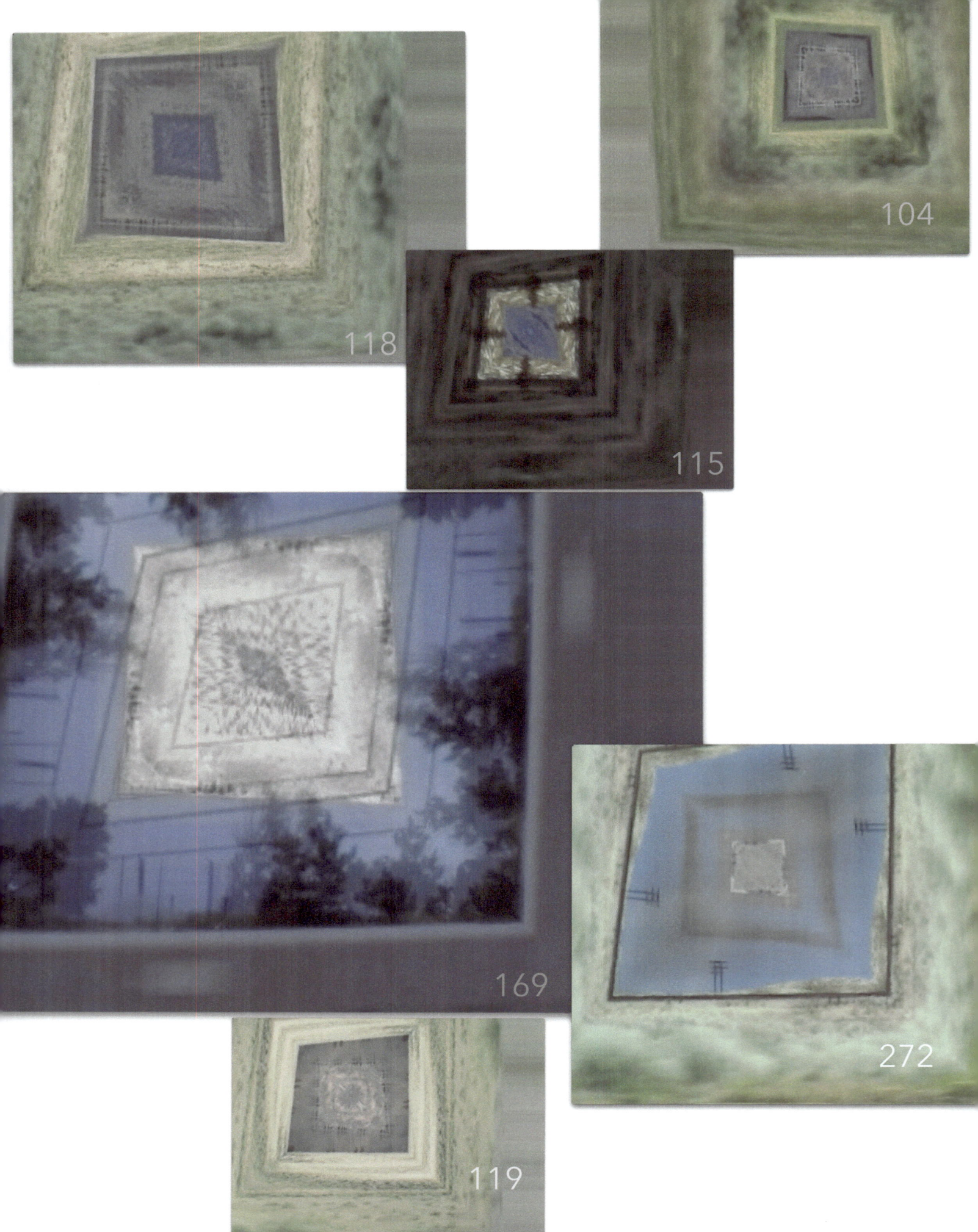

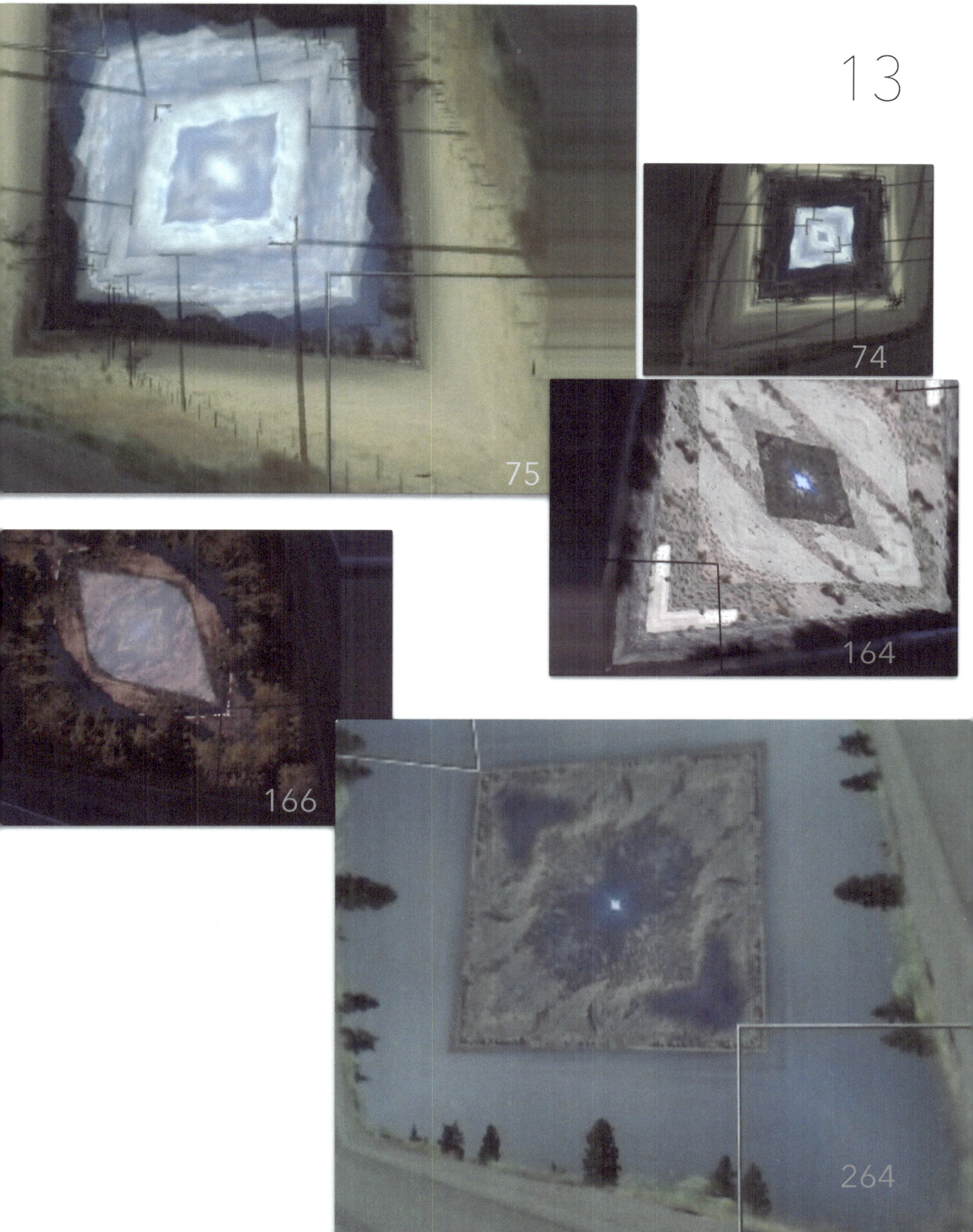

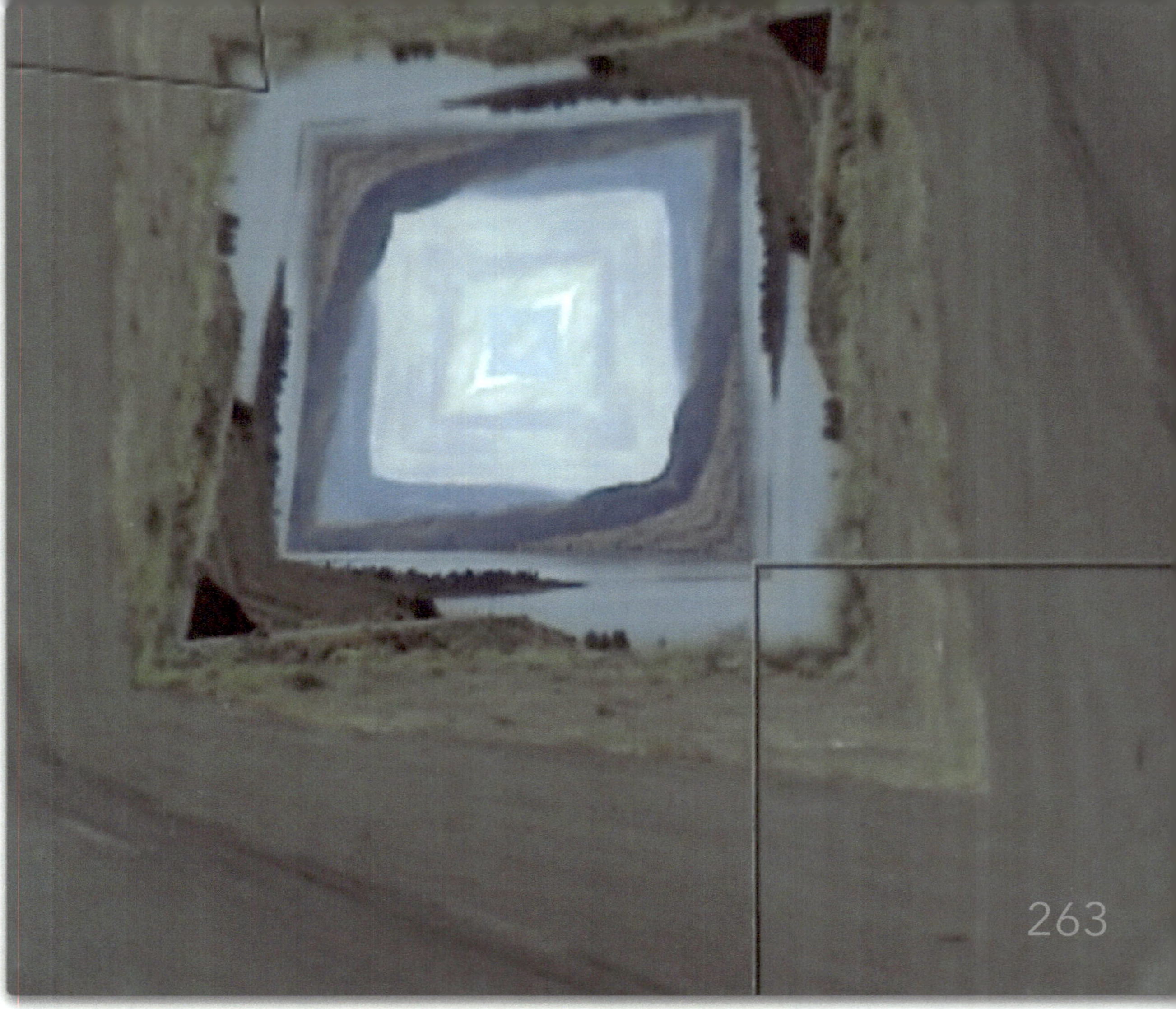

263

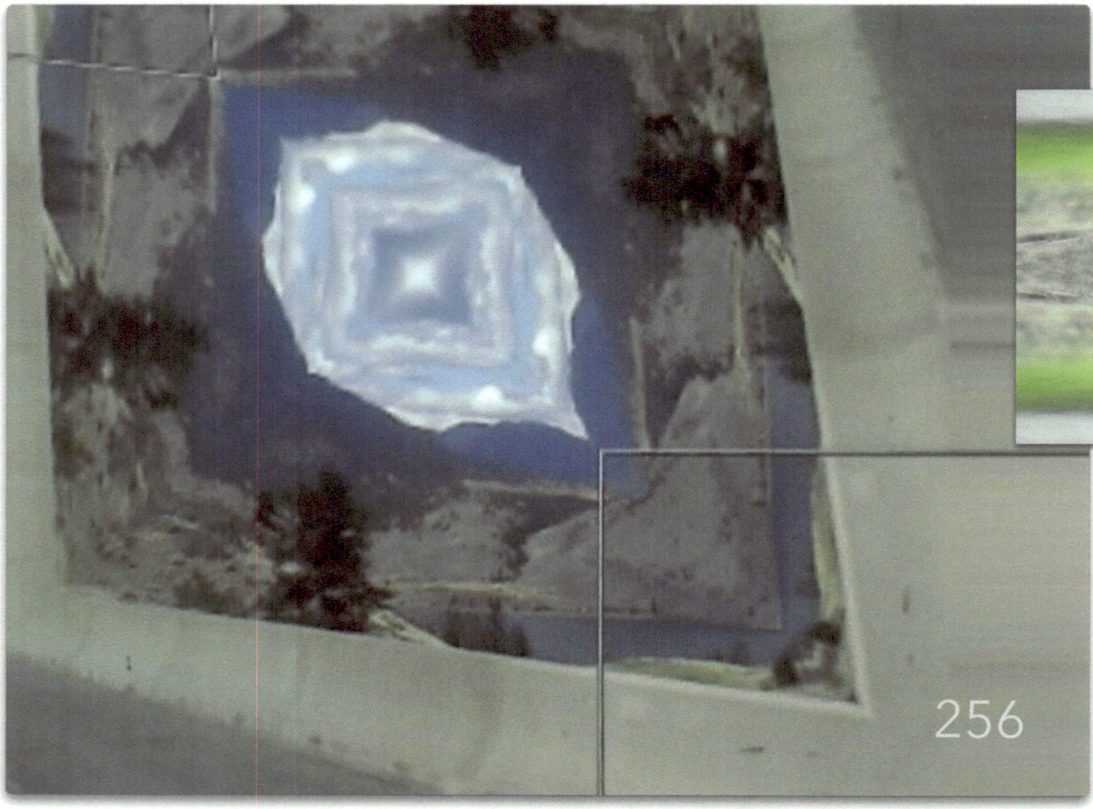

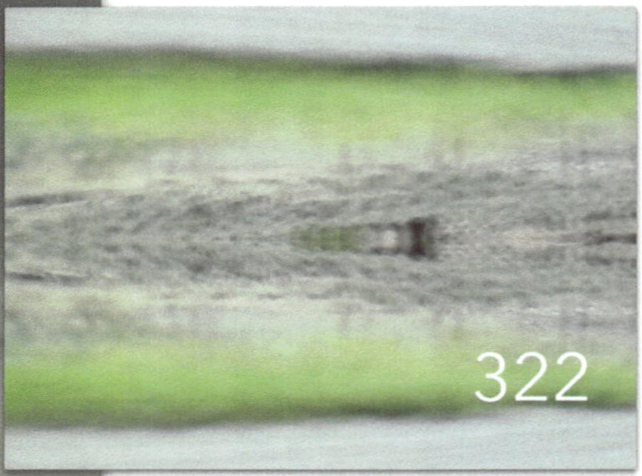

322

256

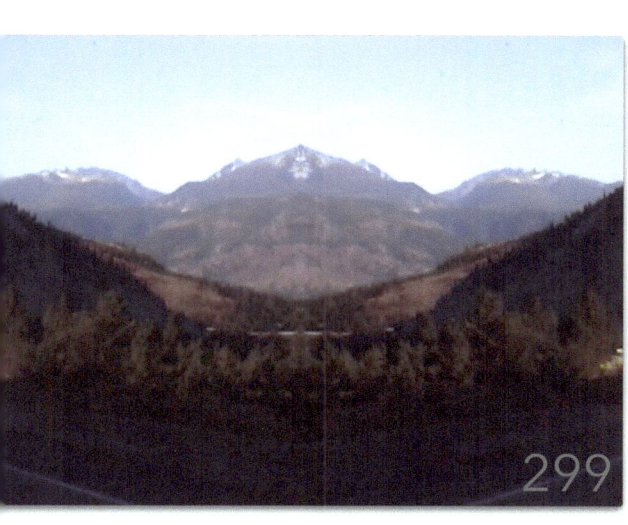

299

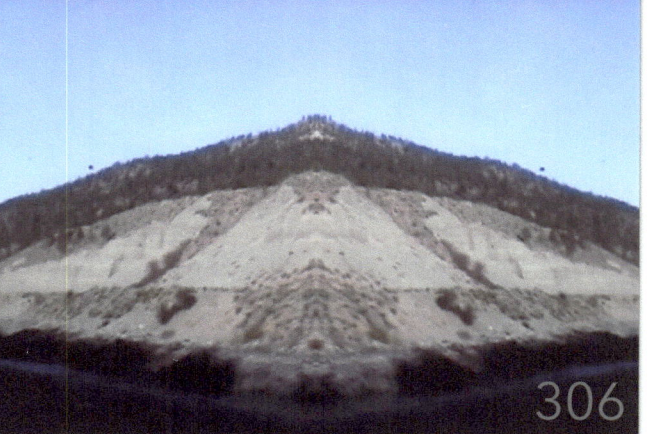

306

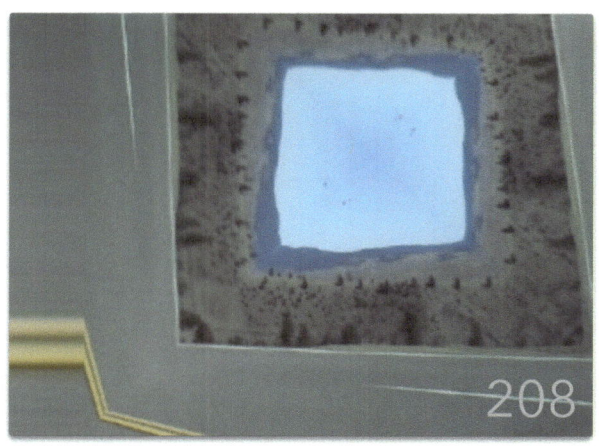

208

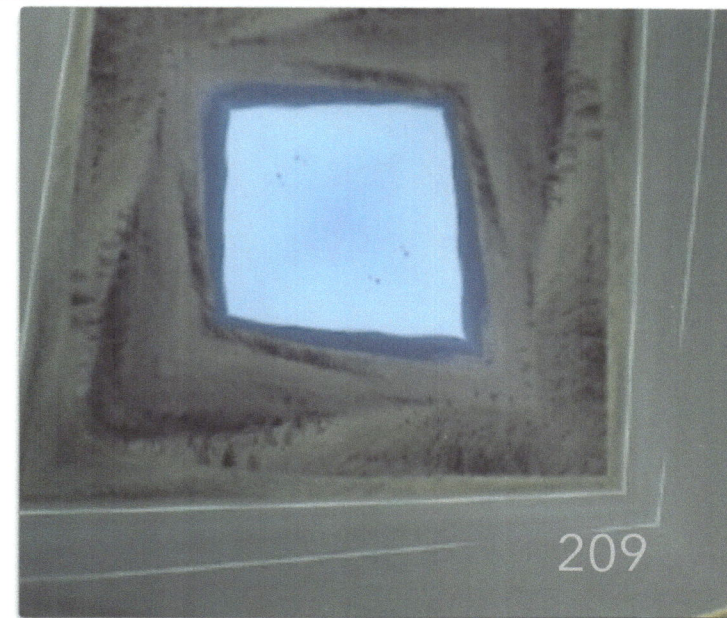

209

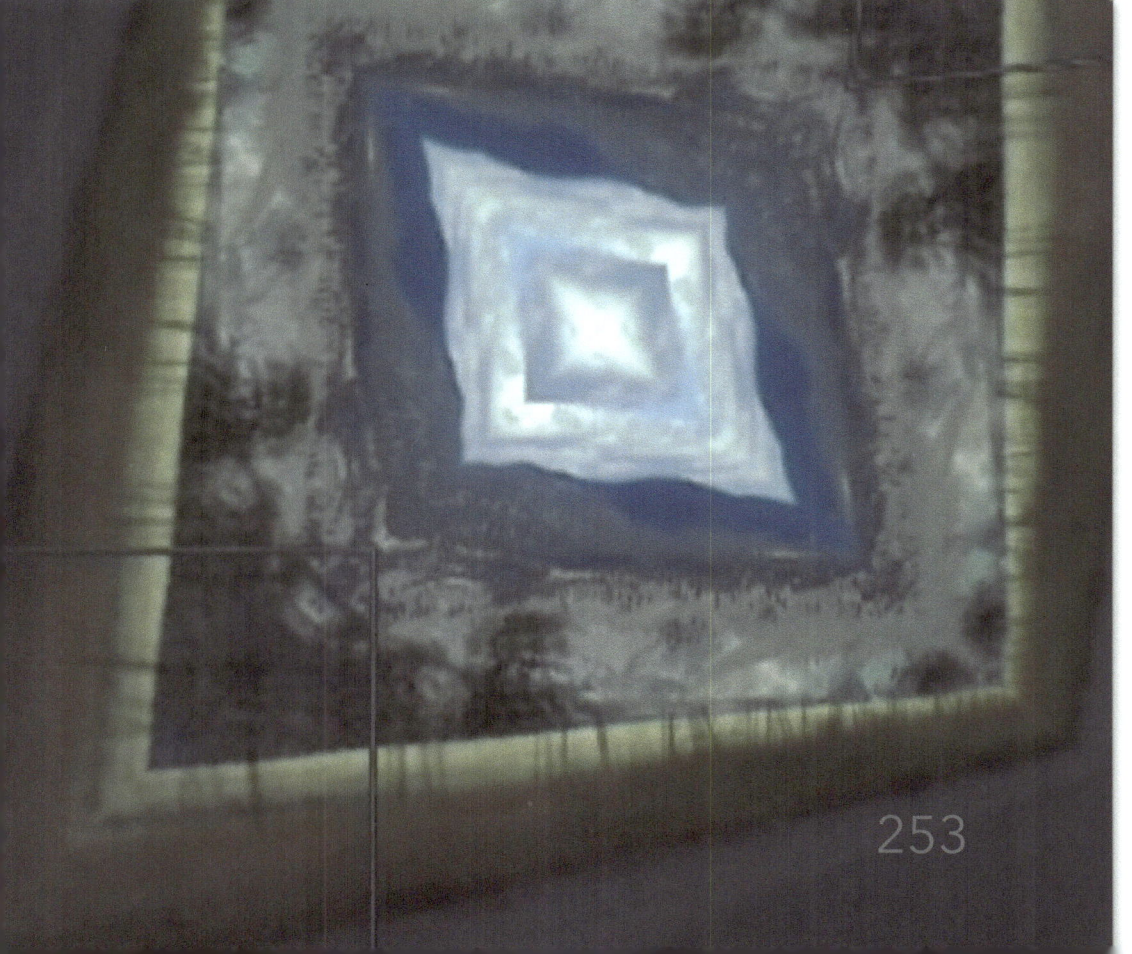

253

dance

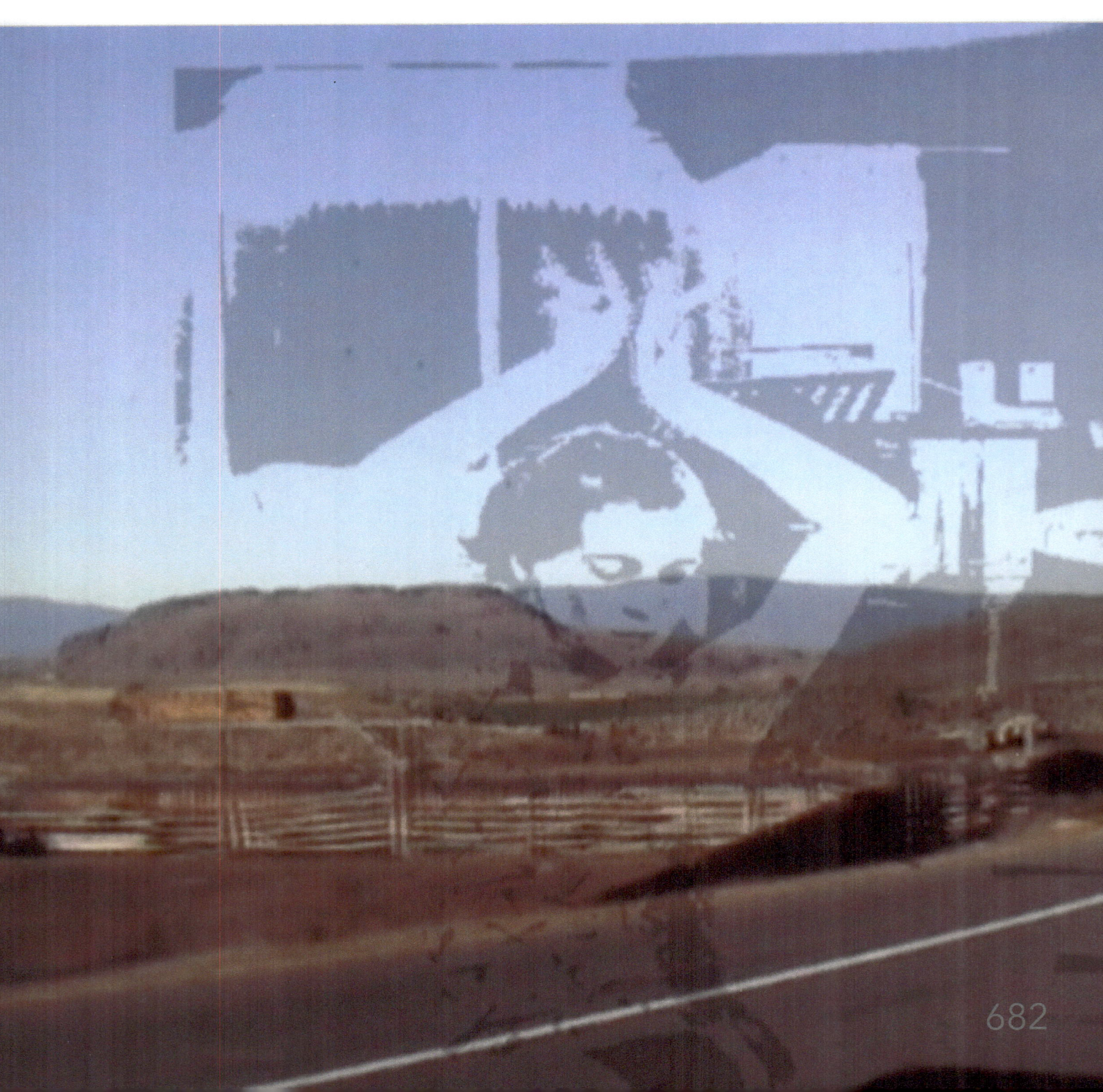

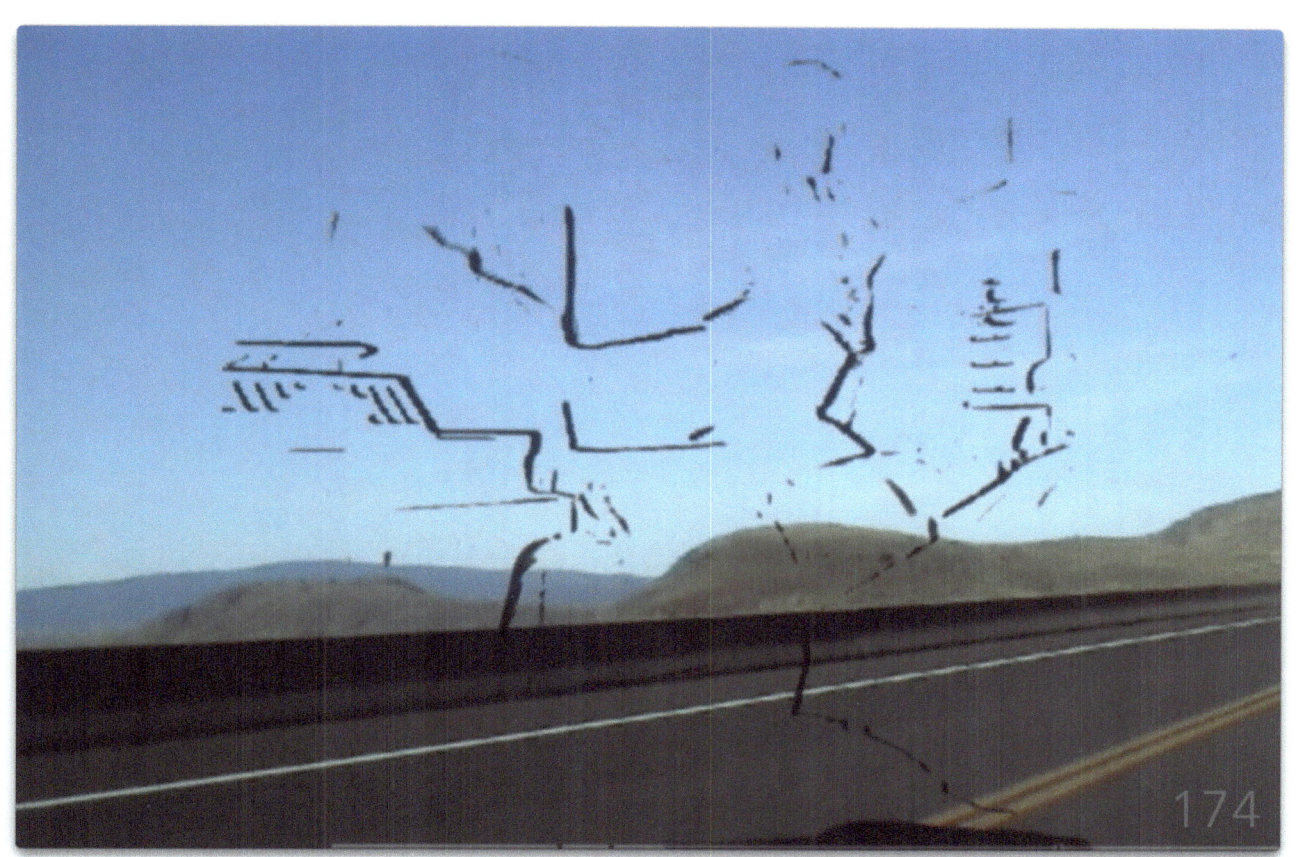

174

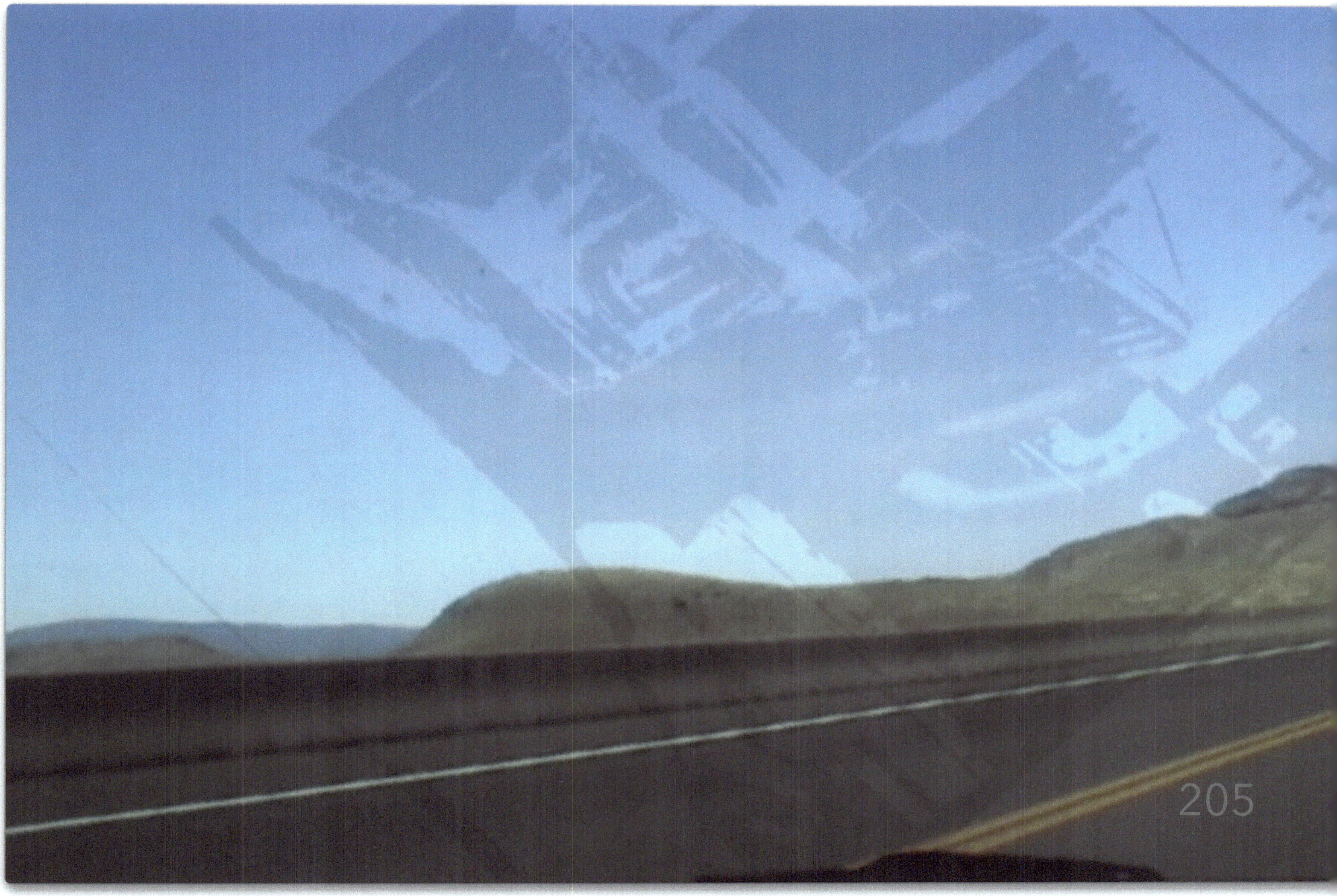

205

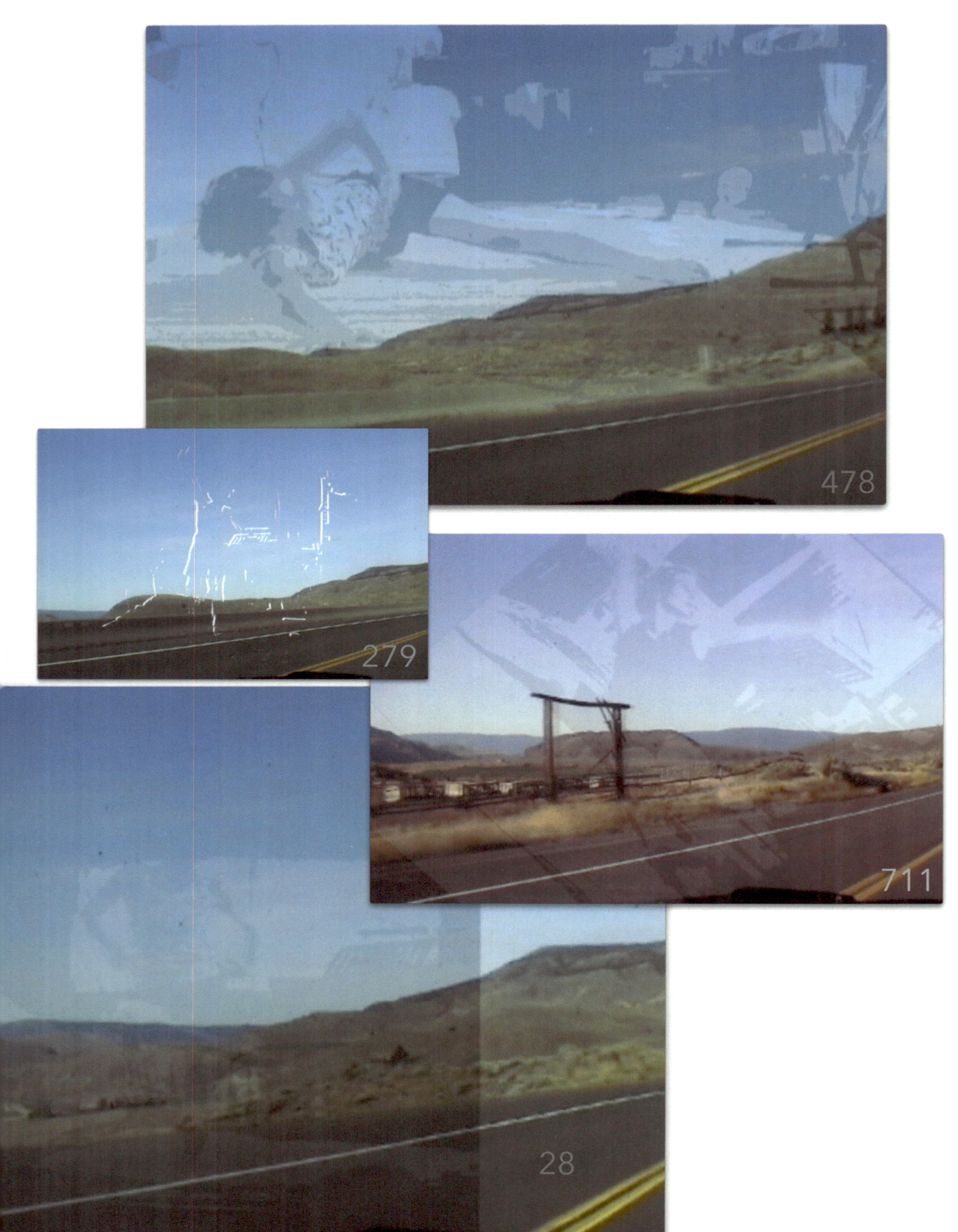

16

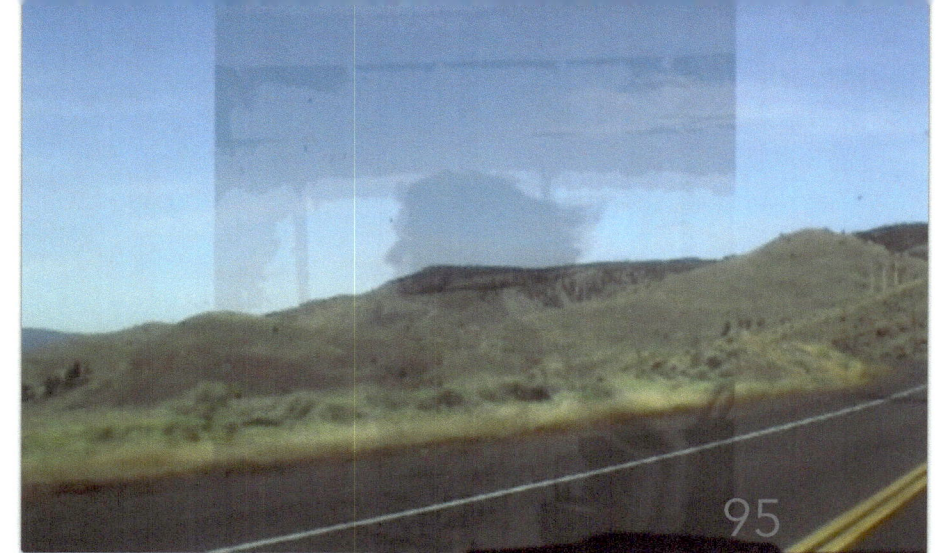

95

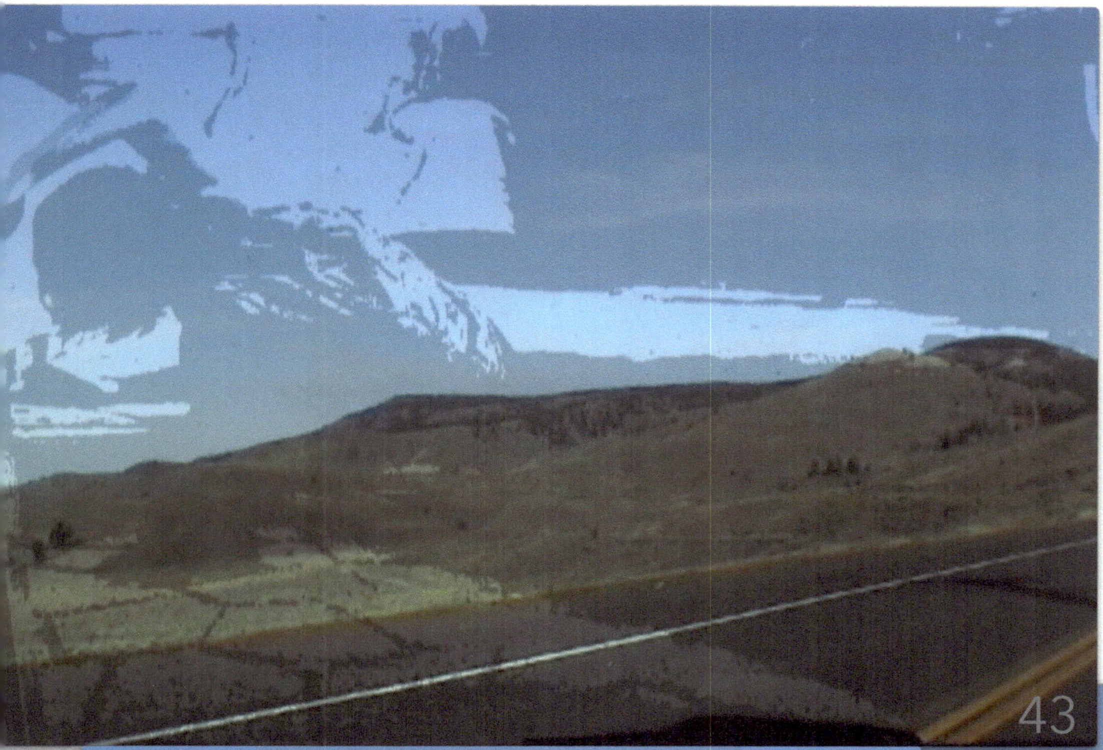

43

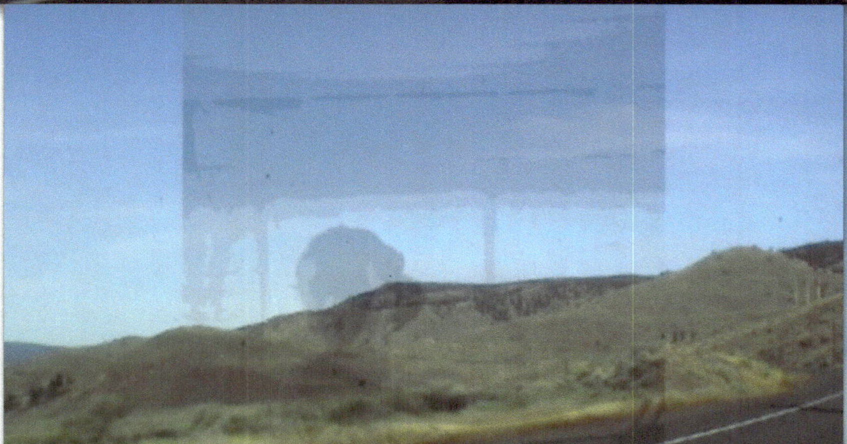

97

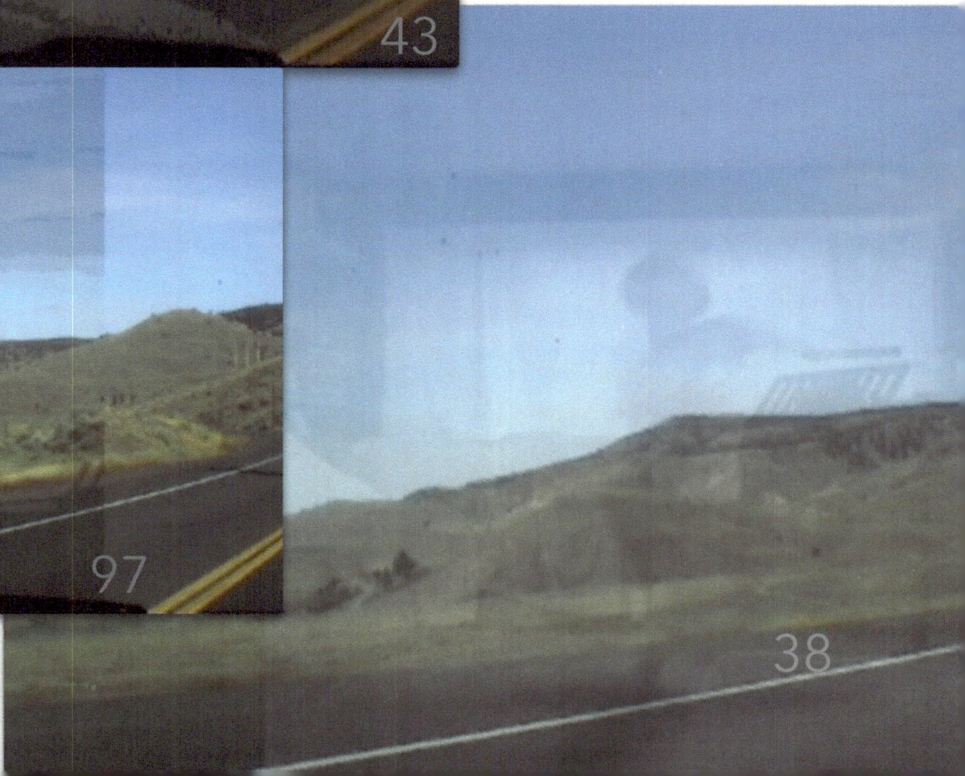

38

desert

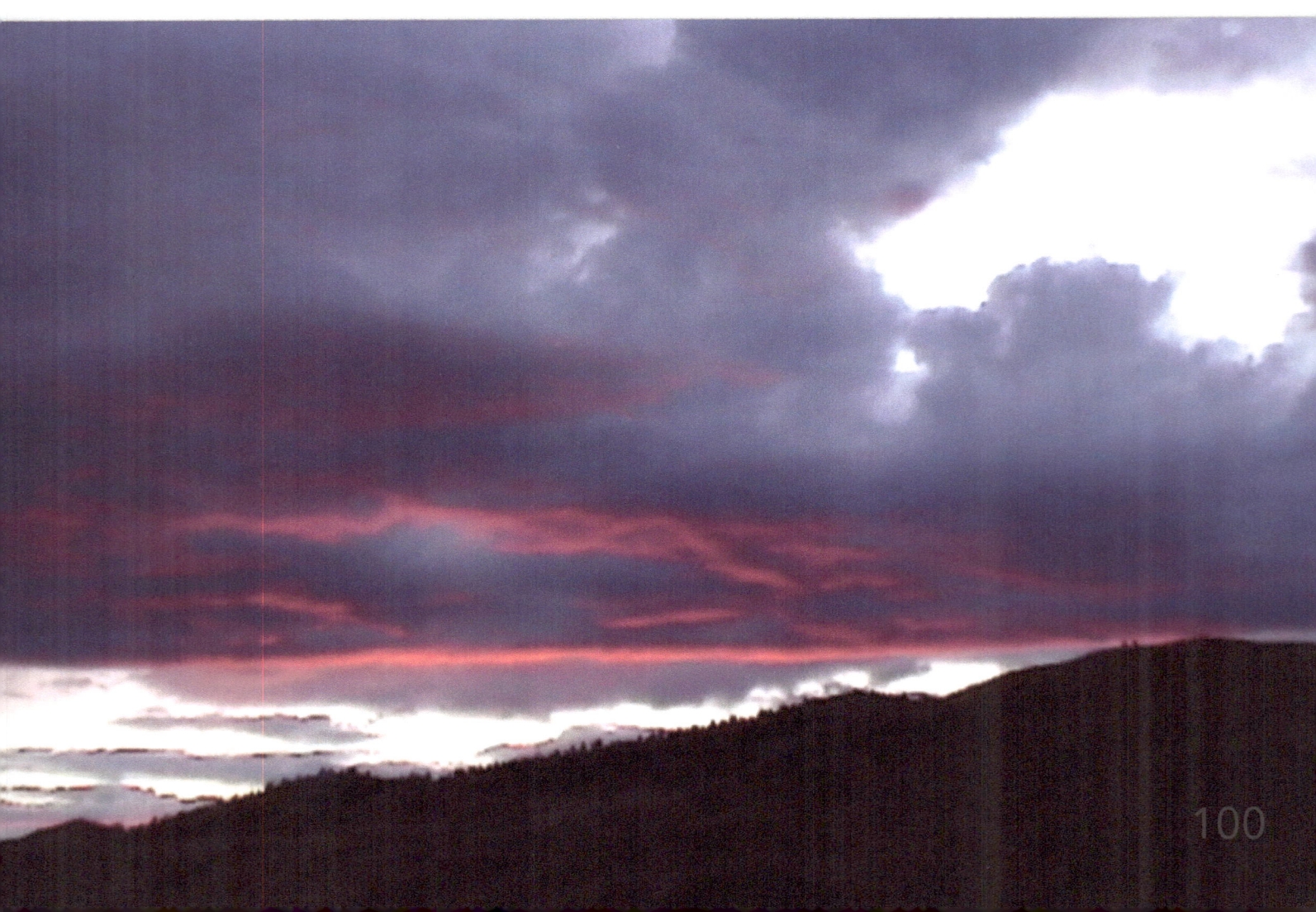

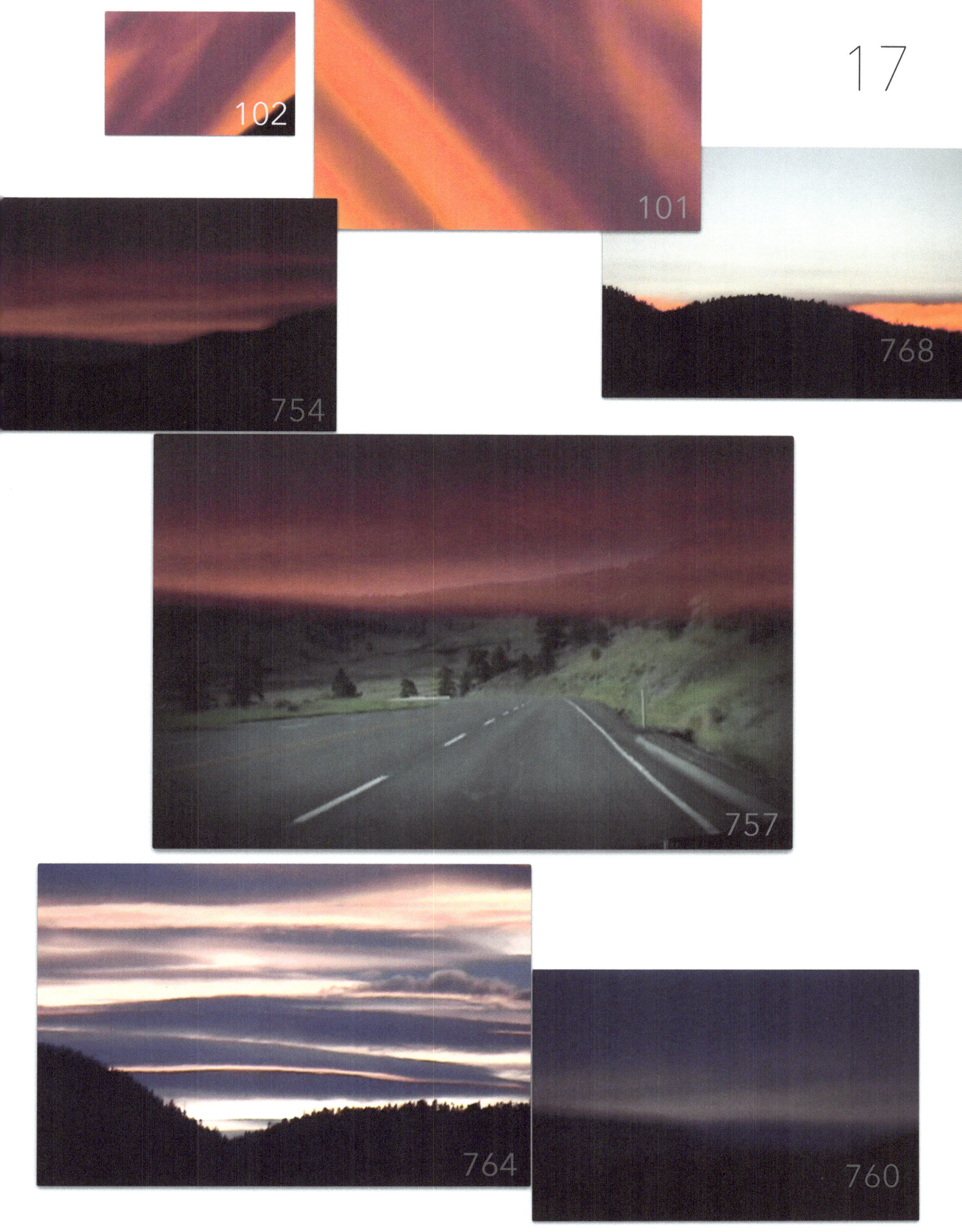

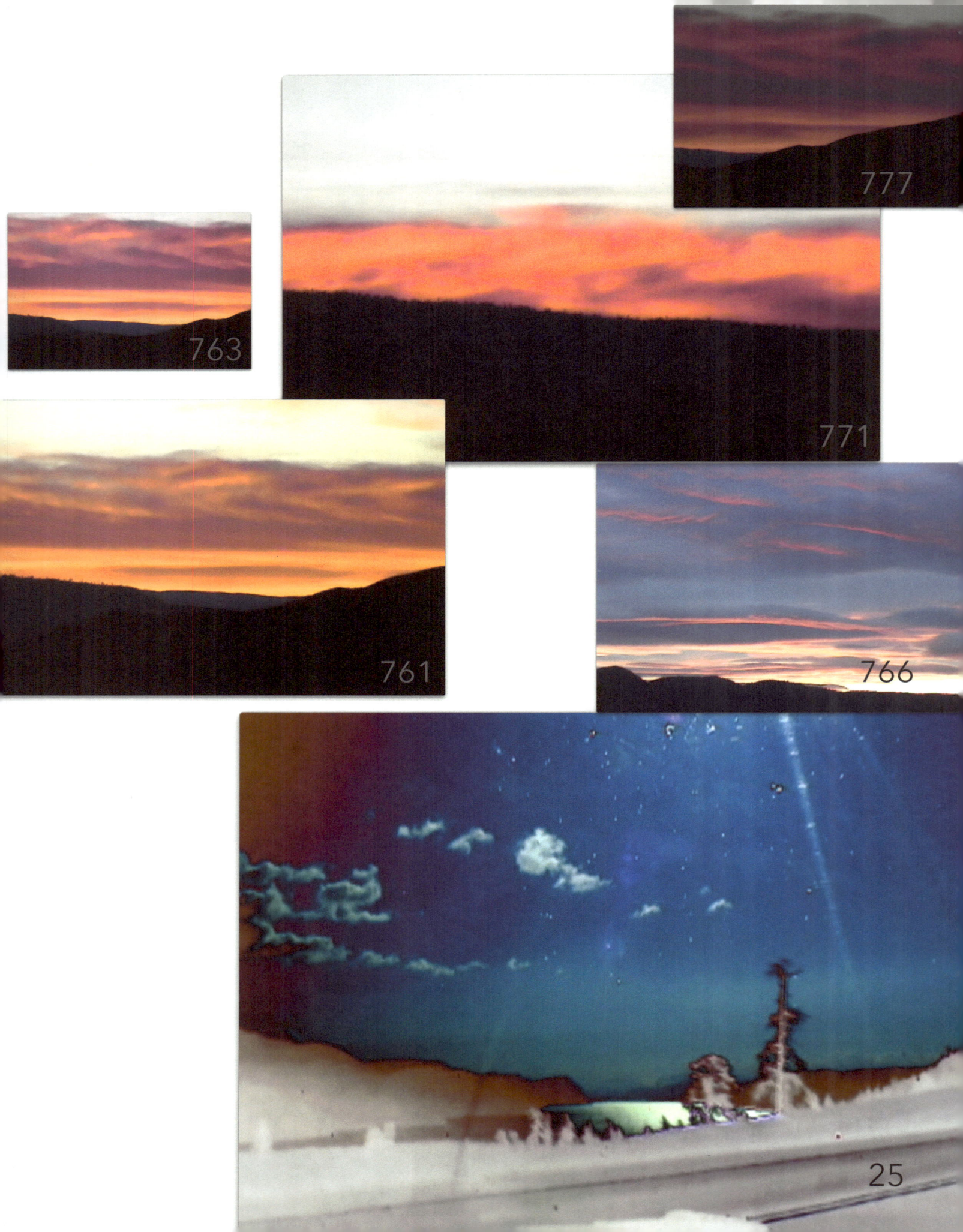

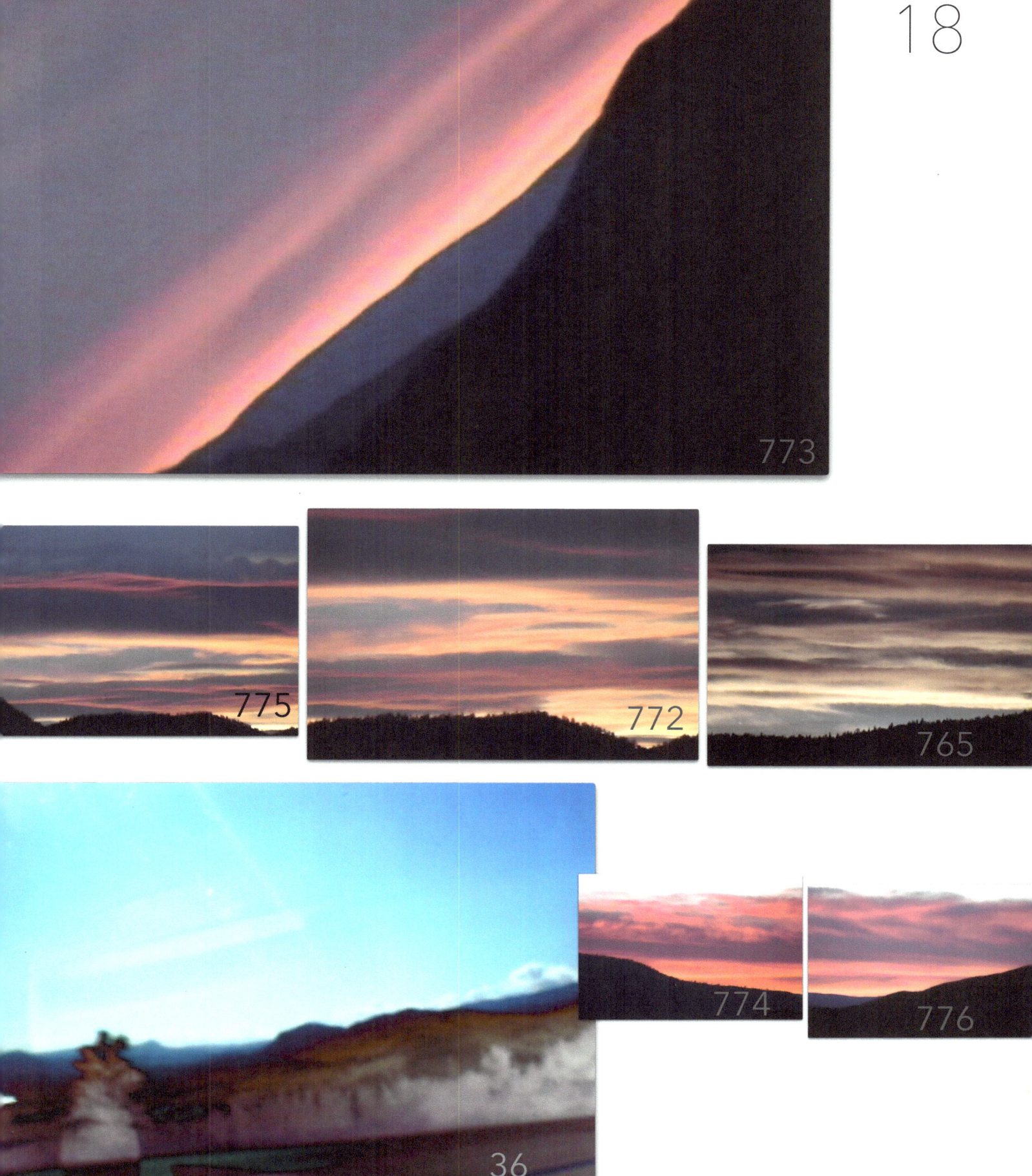

773

775

772

765

36

774

776

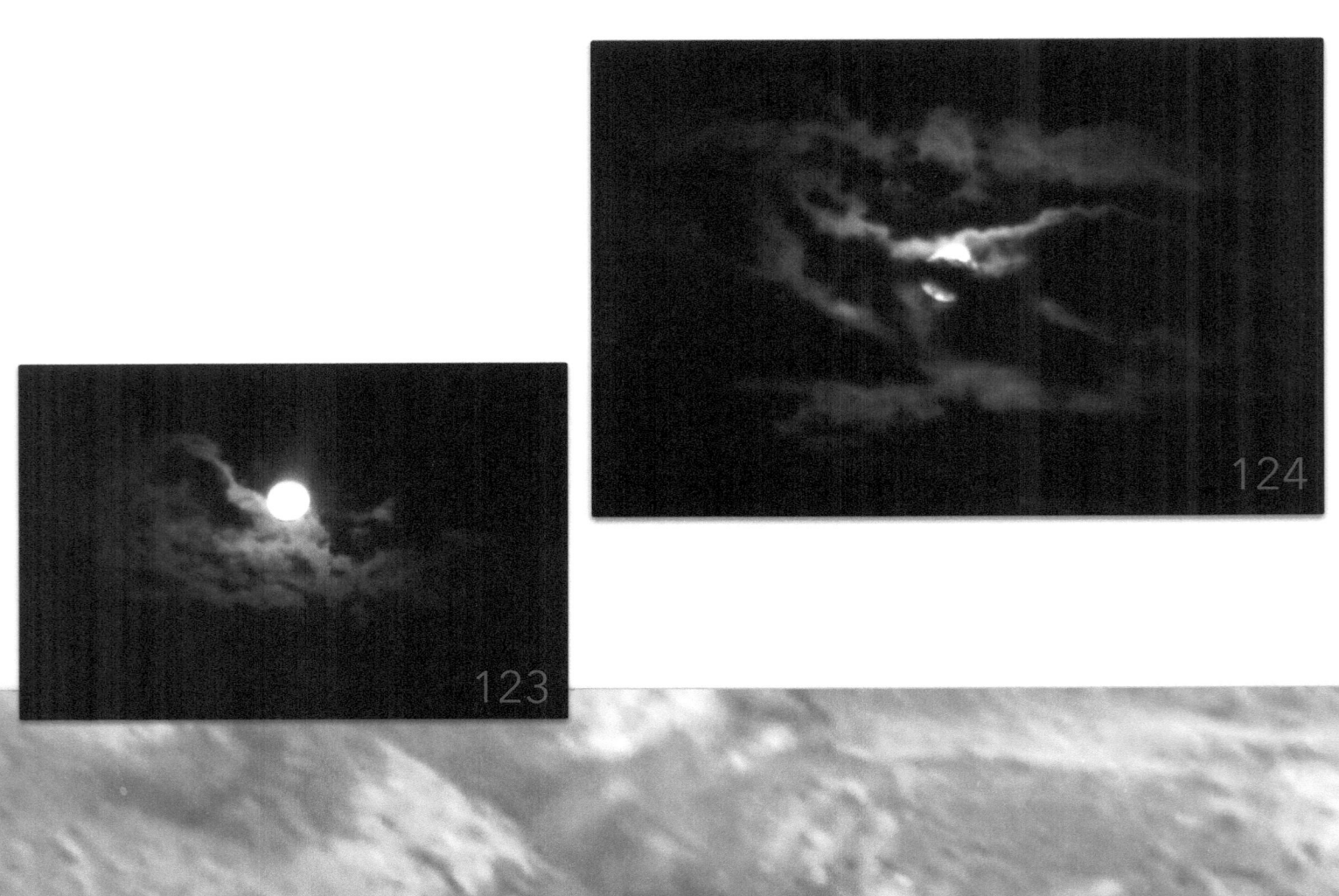

123

124

121

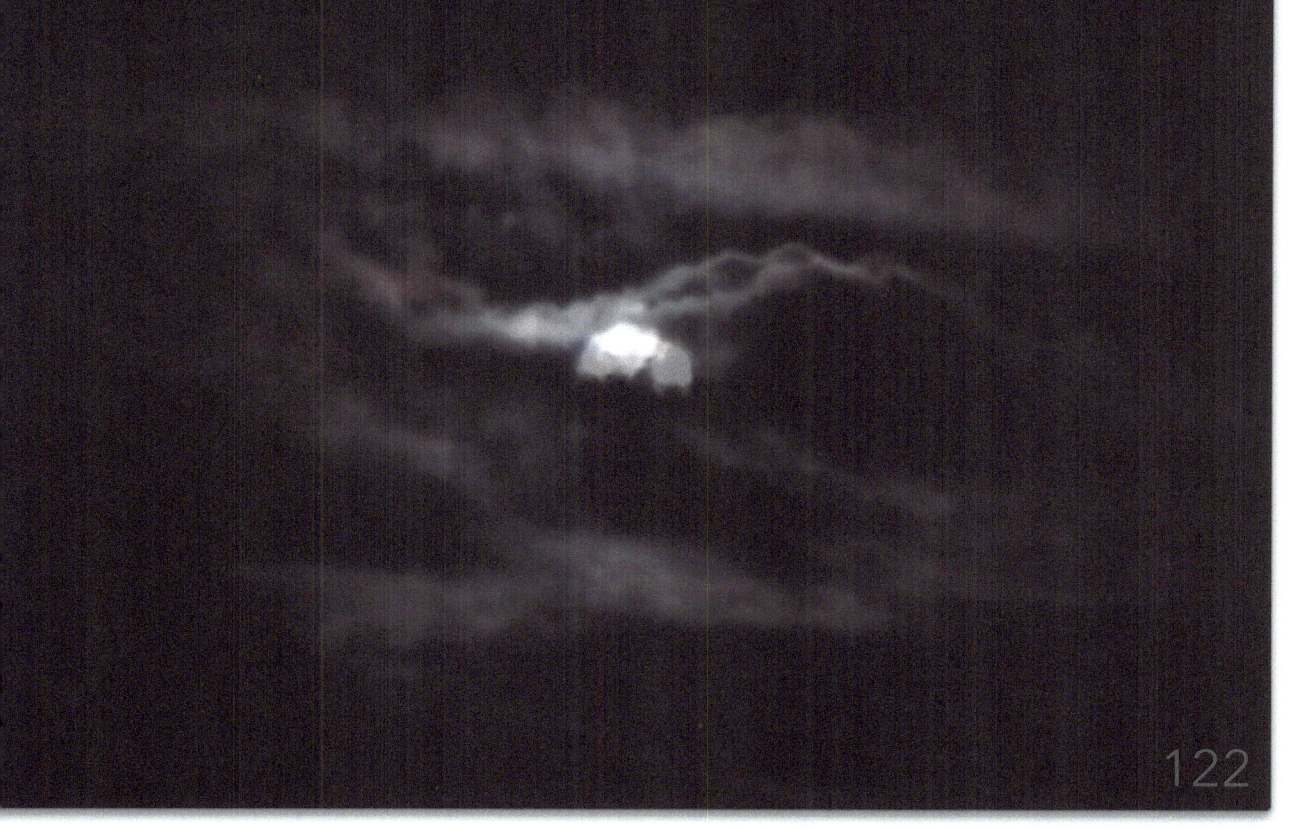

122

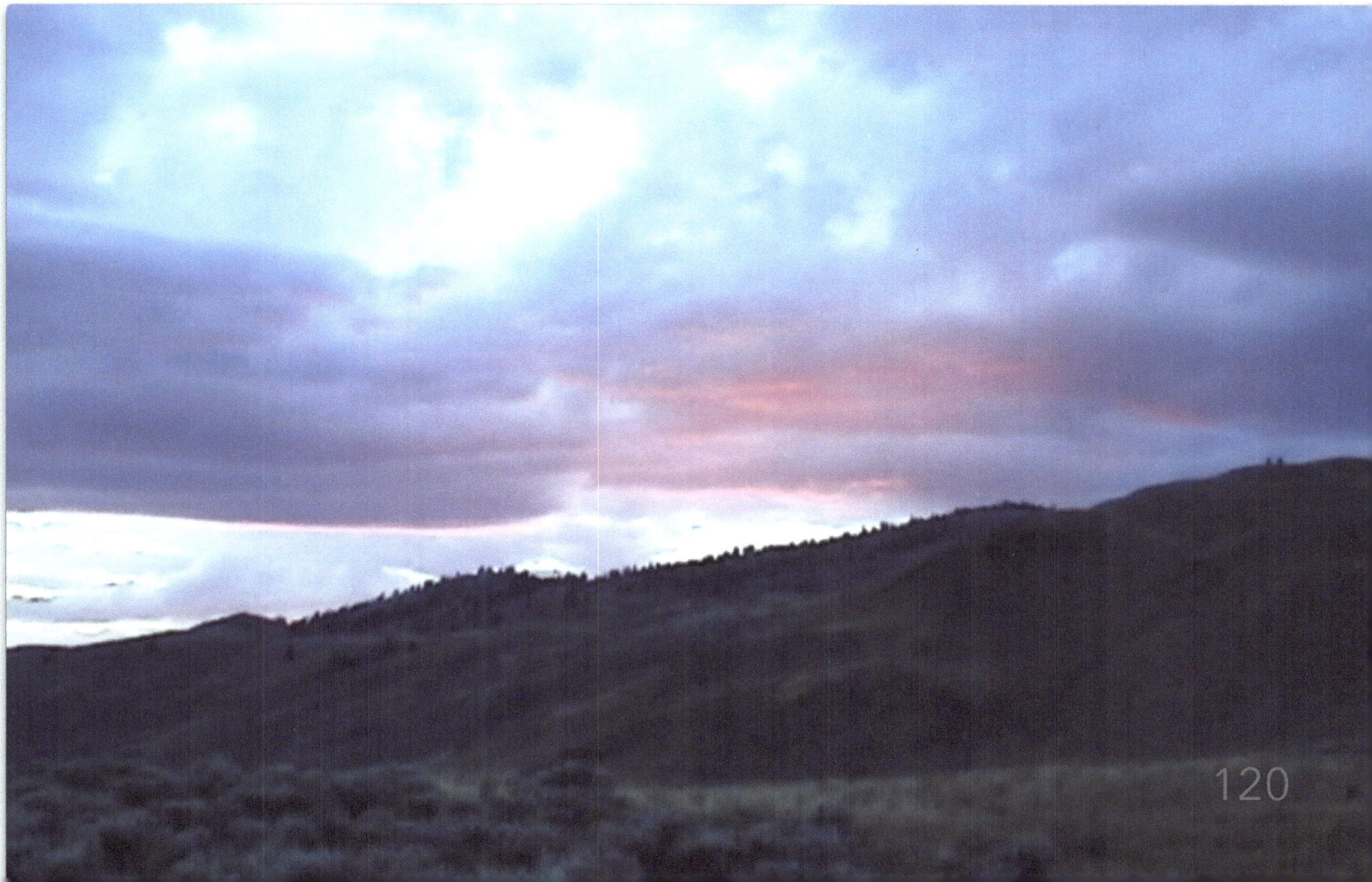

120

vibrant

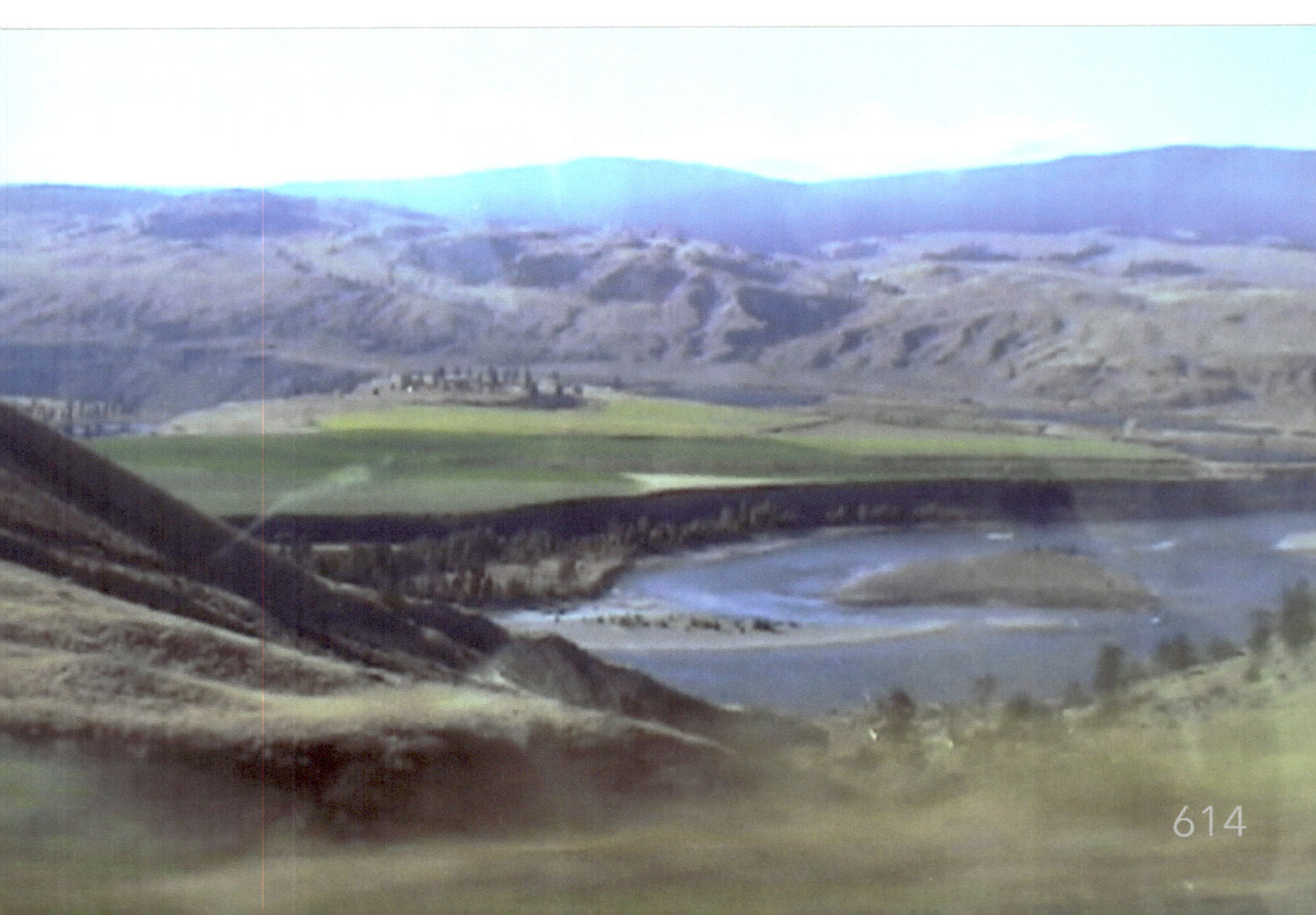

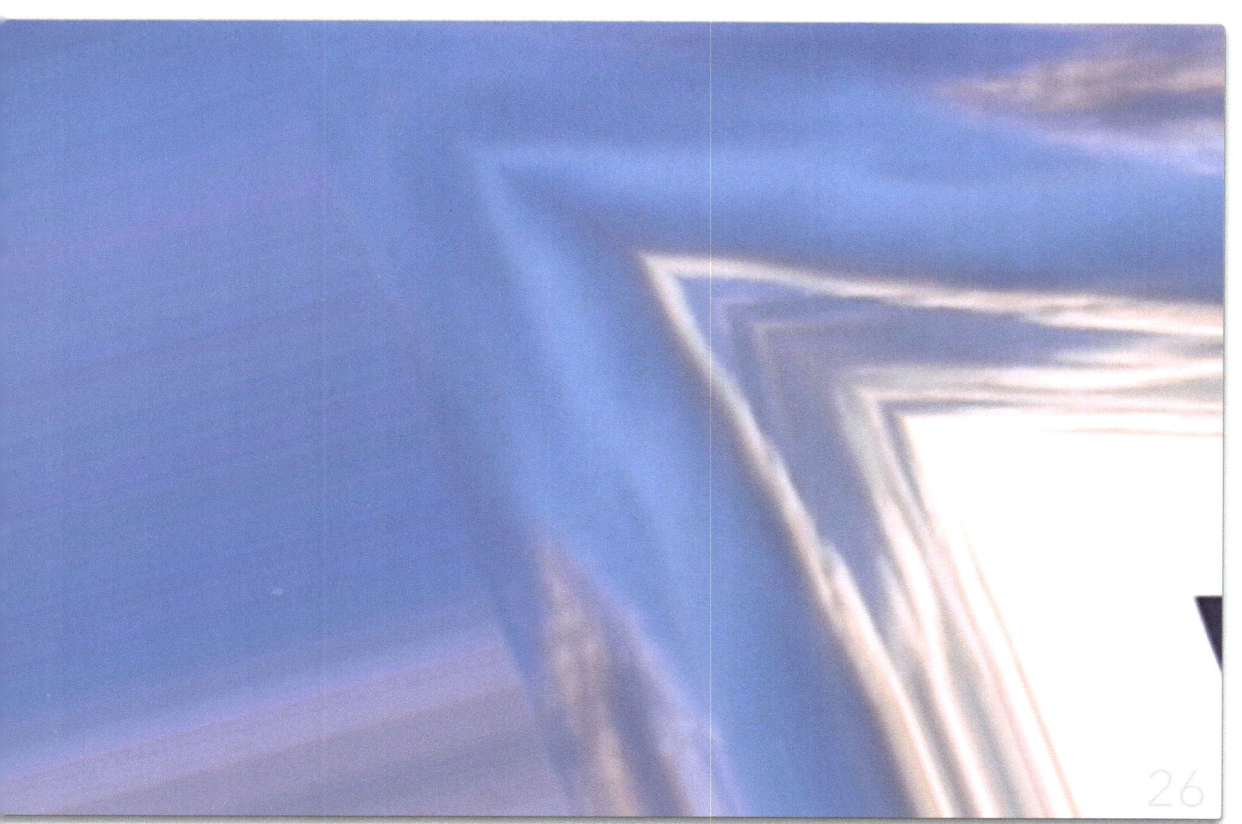

26

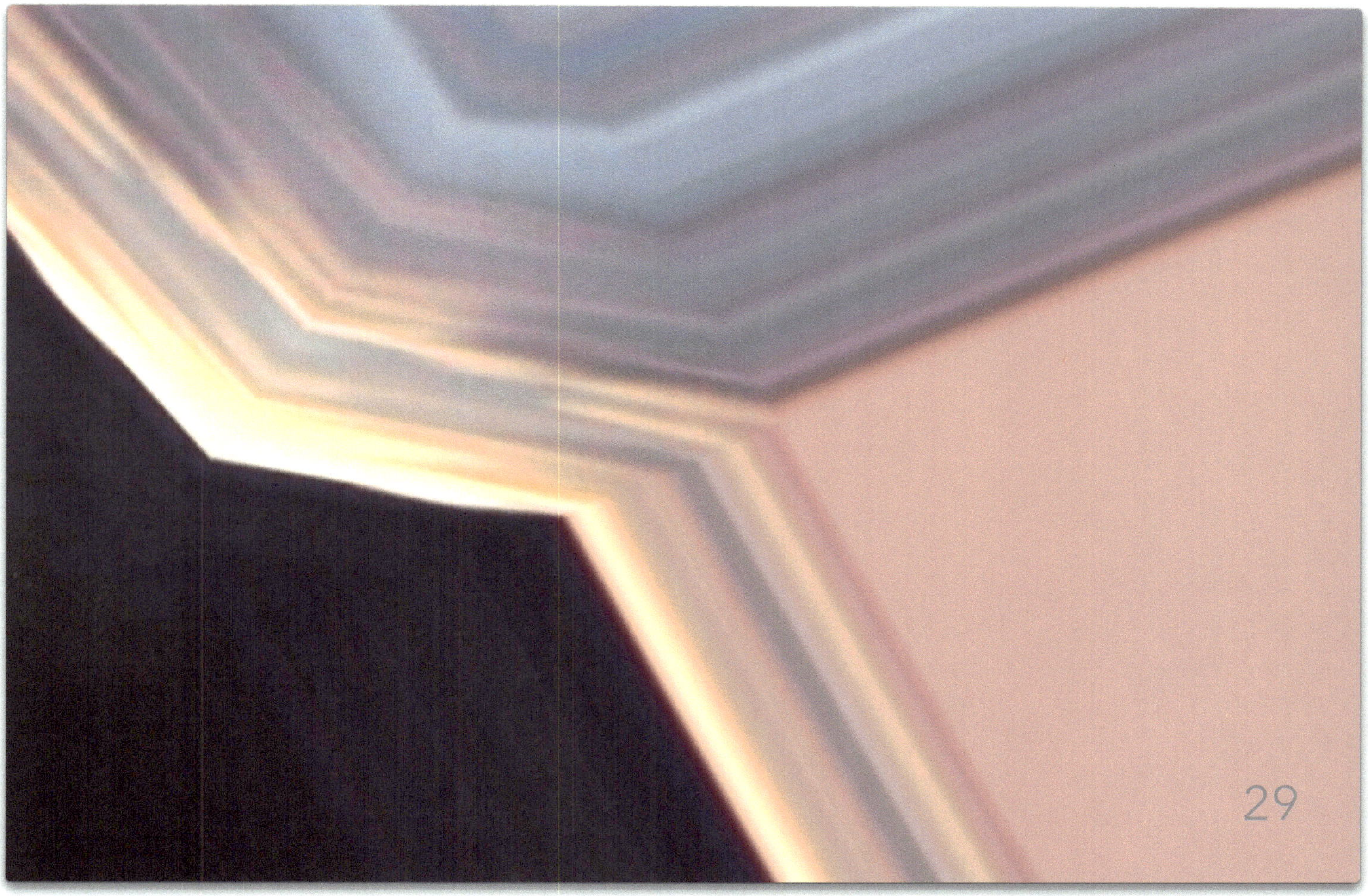

29

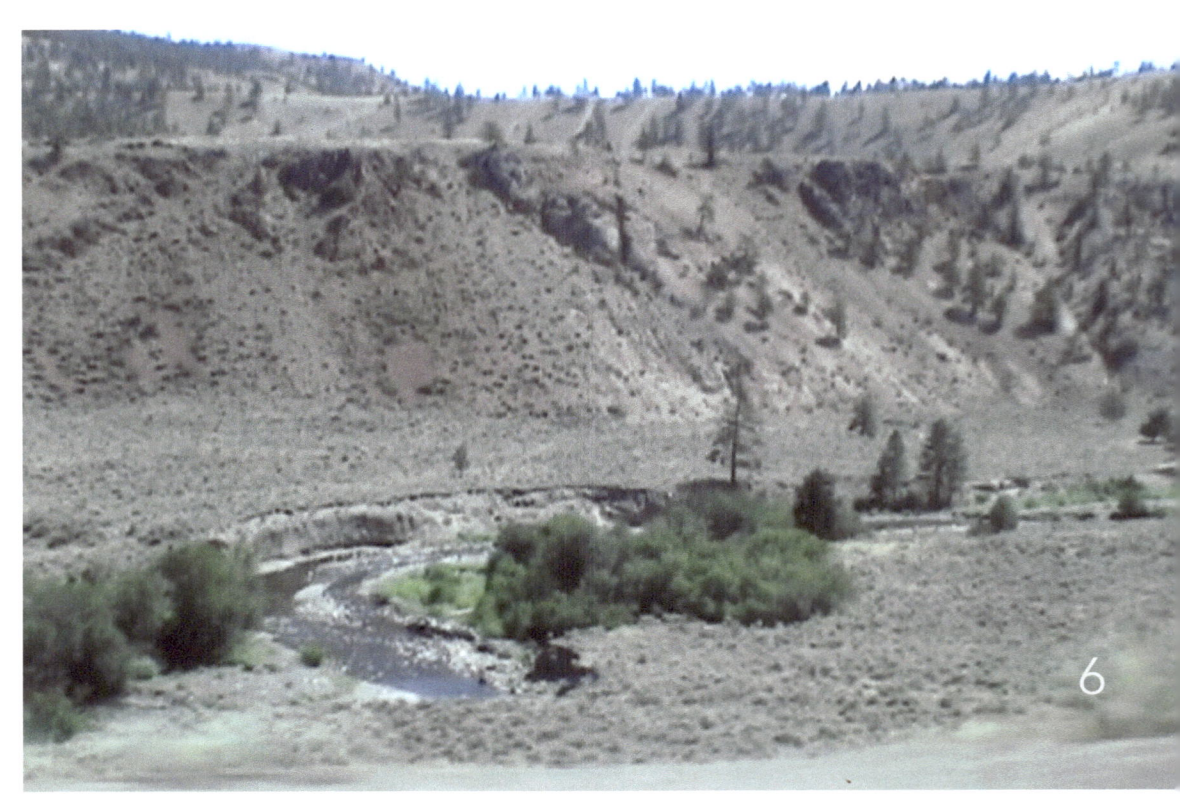

6

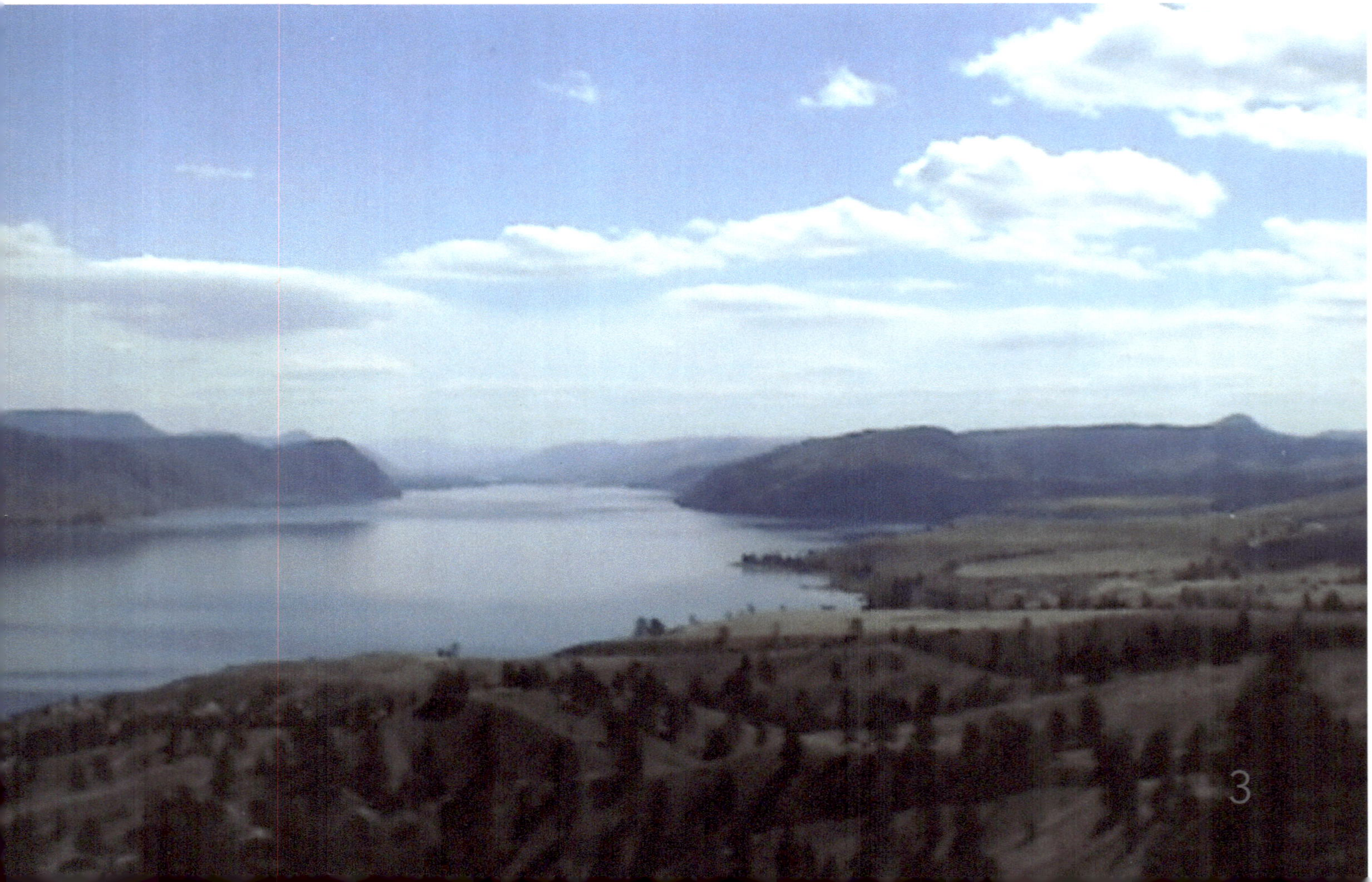

3

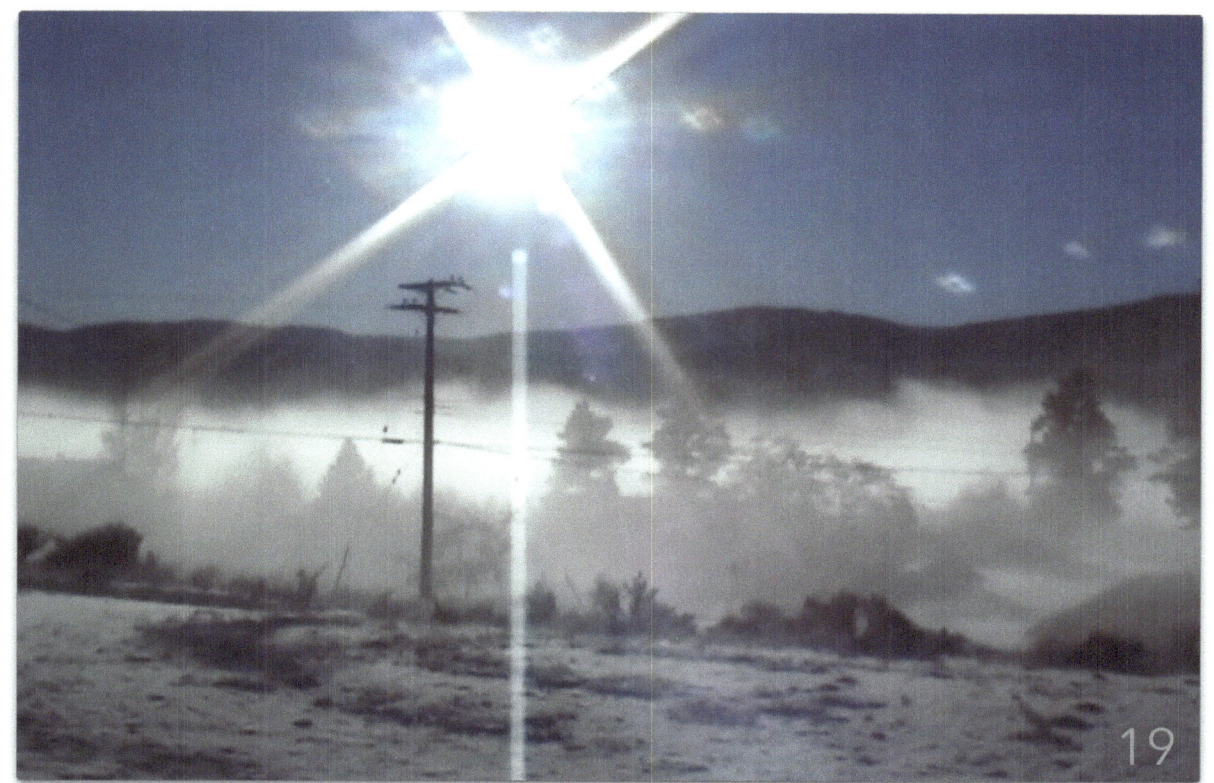

19

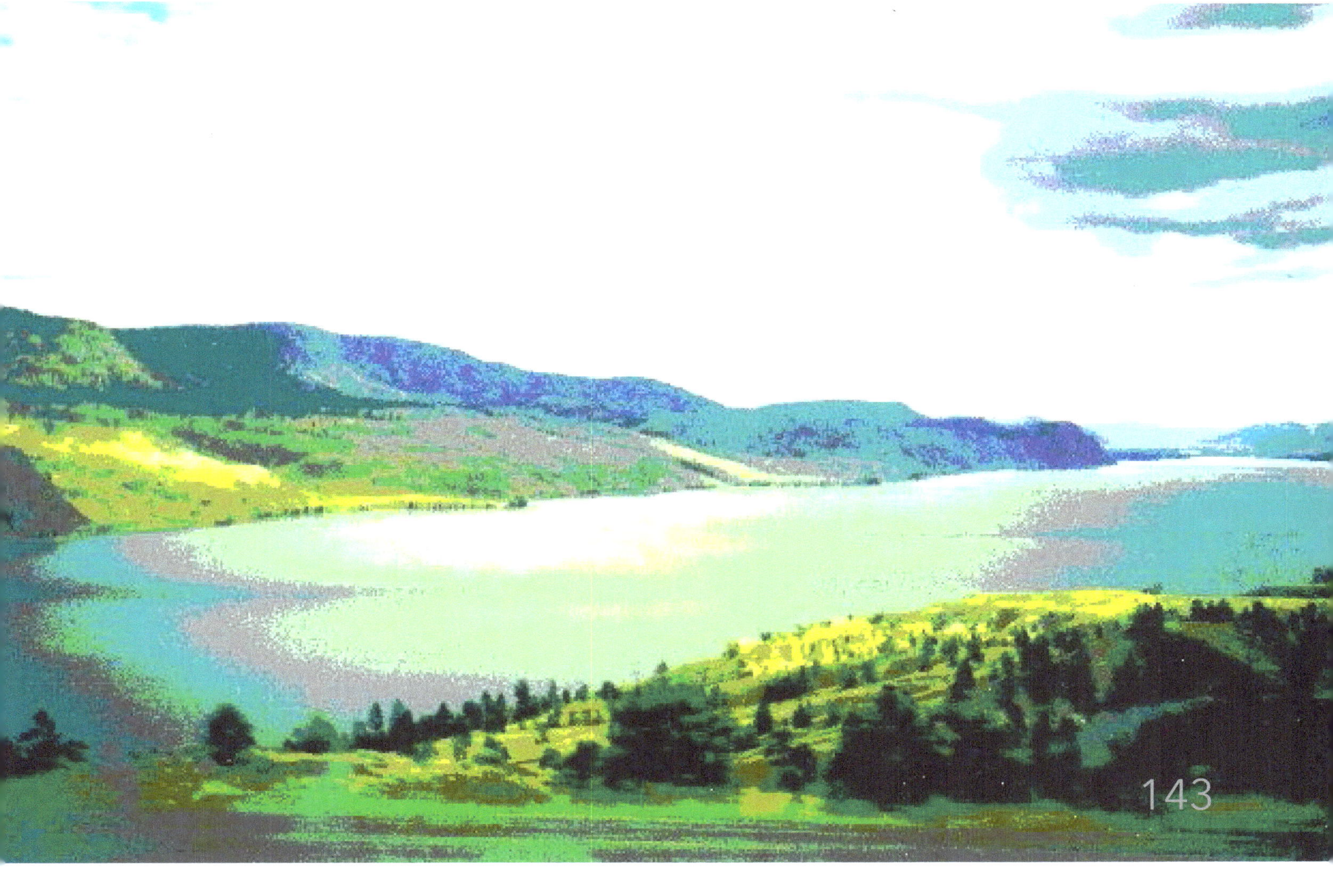

143

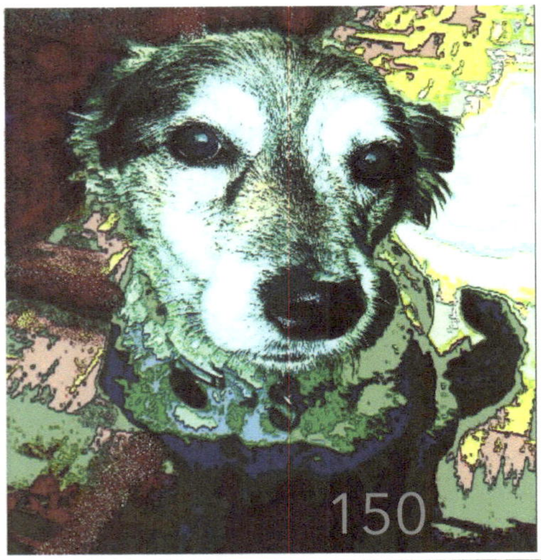

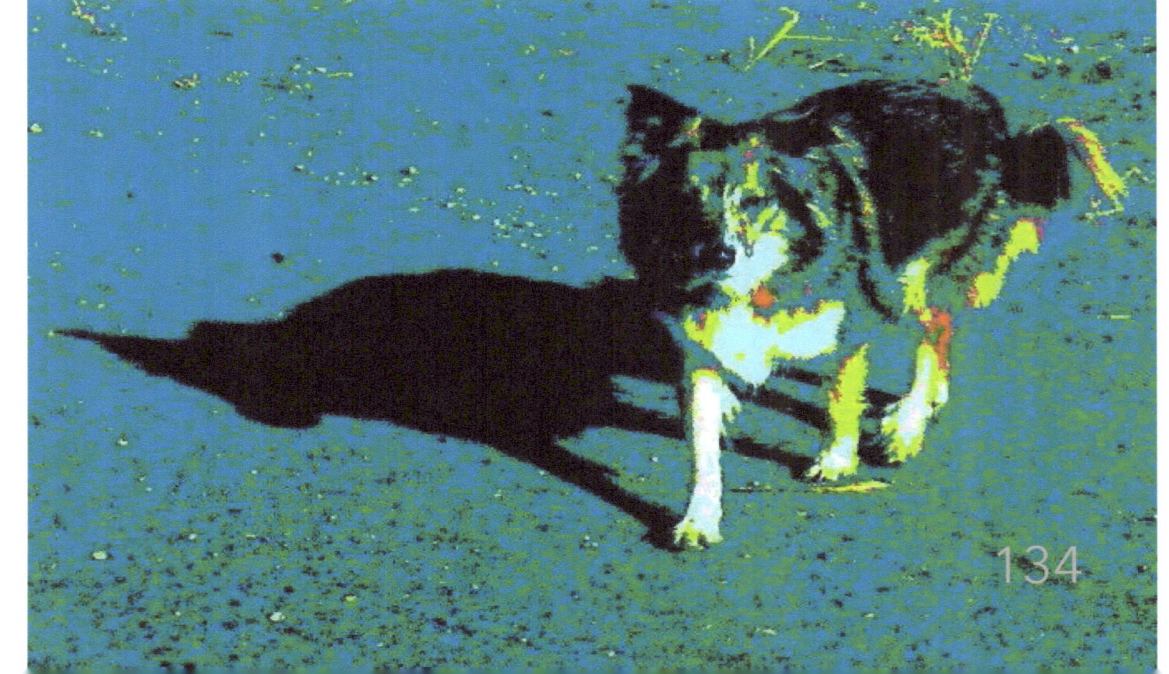

150

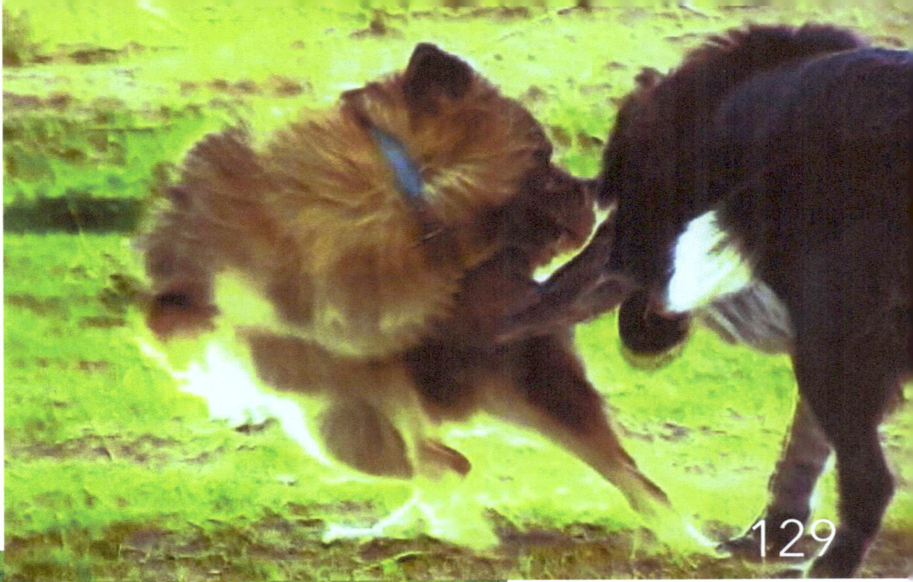

129

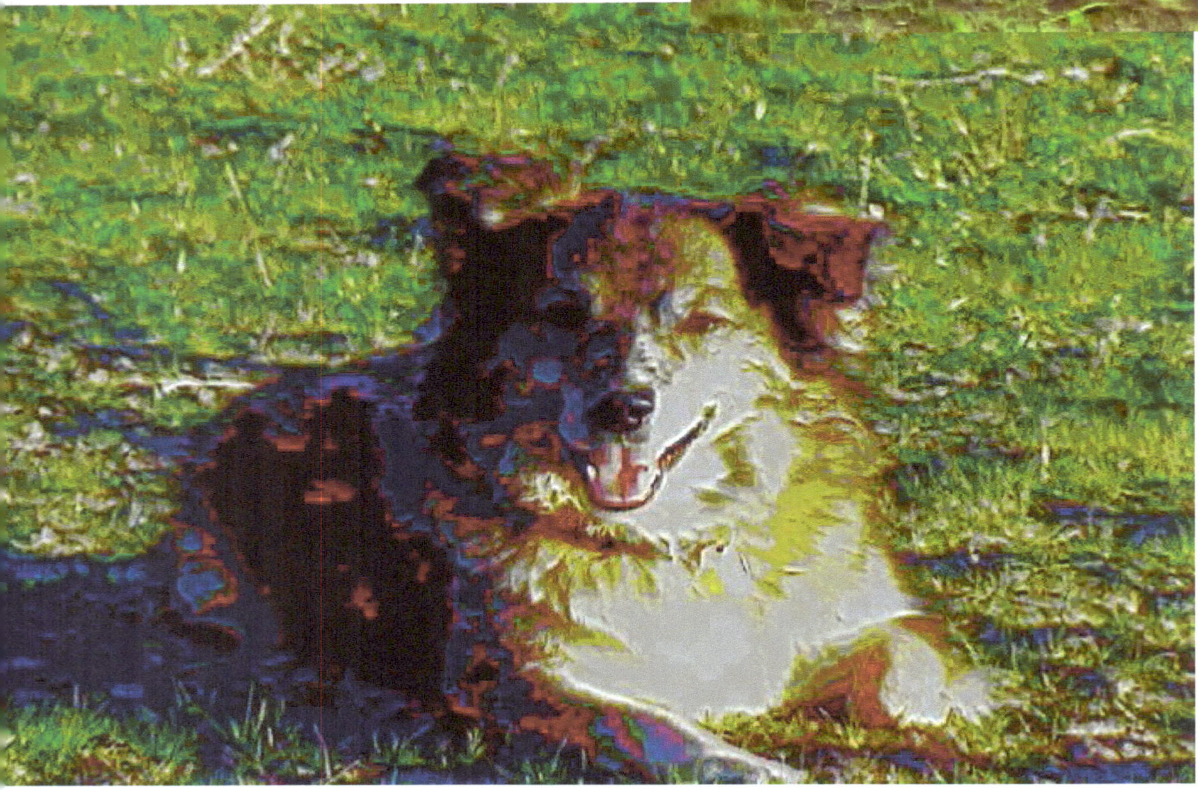

140

134

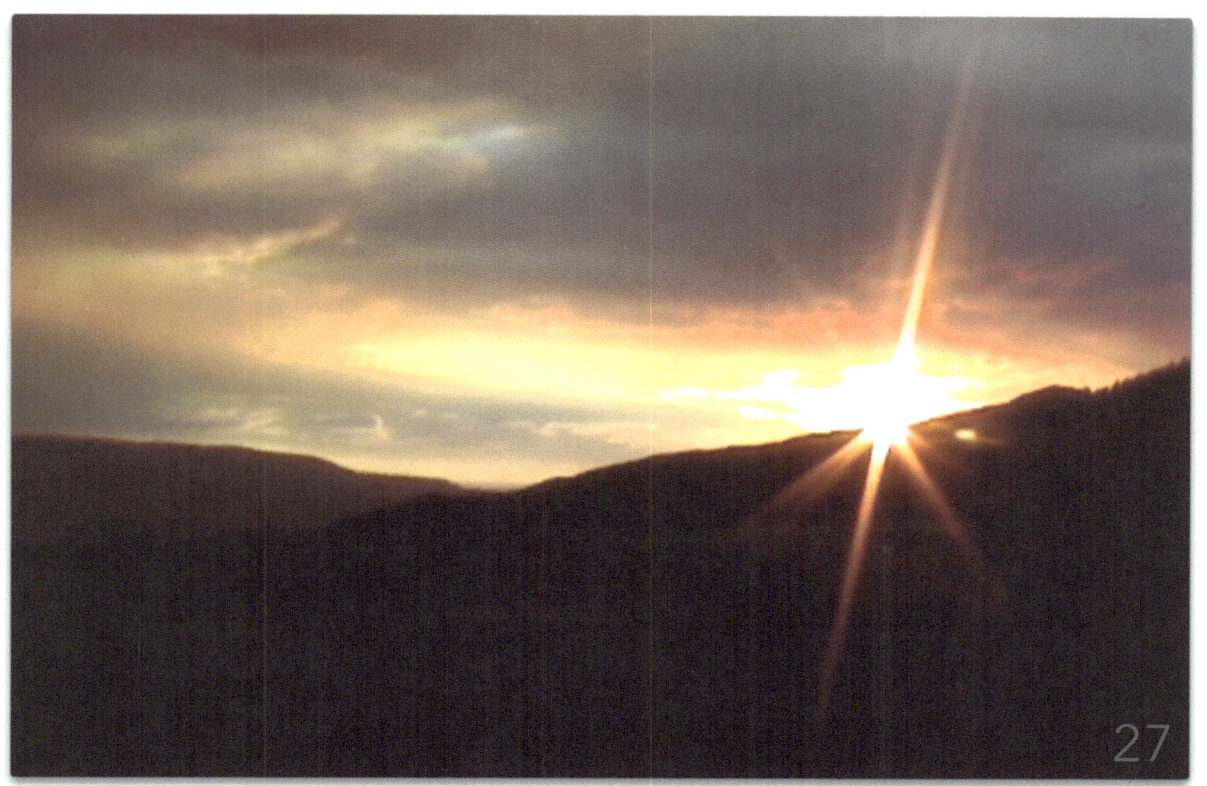

27

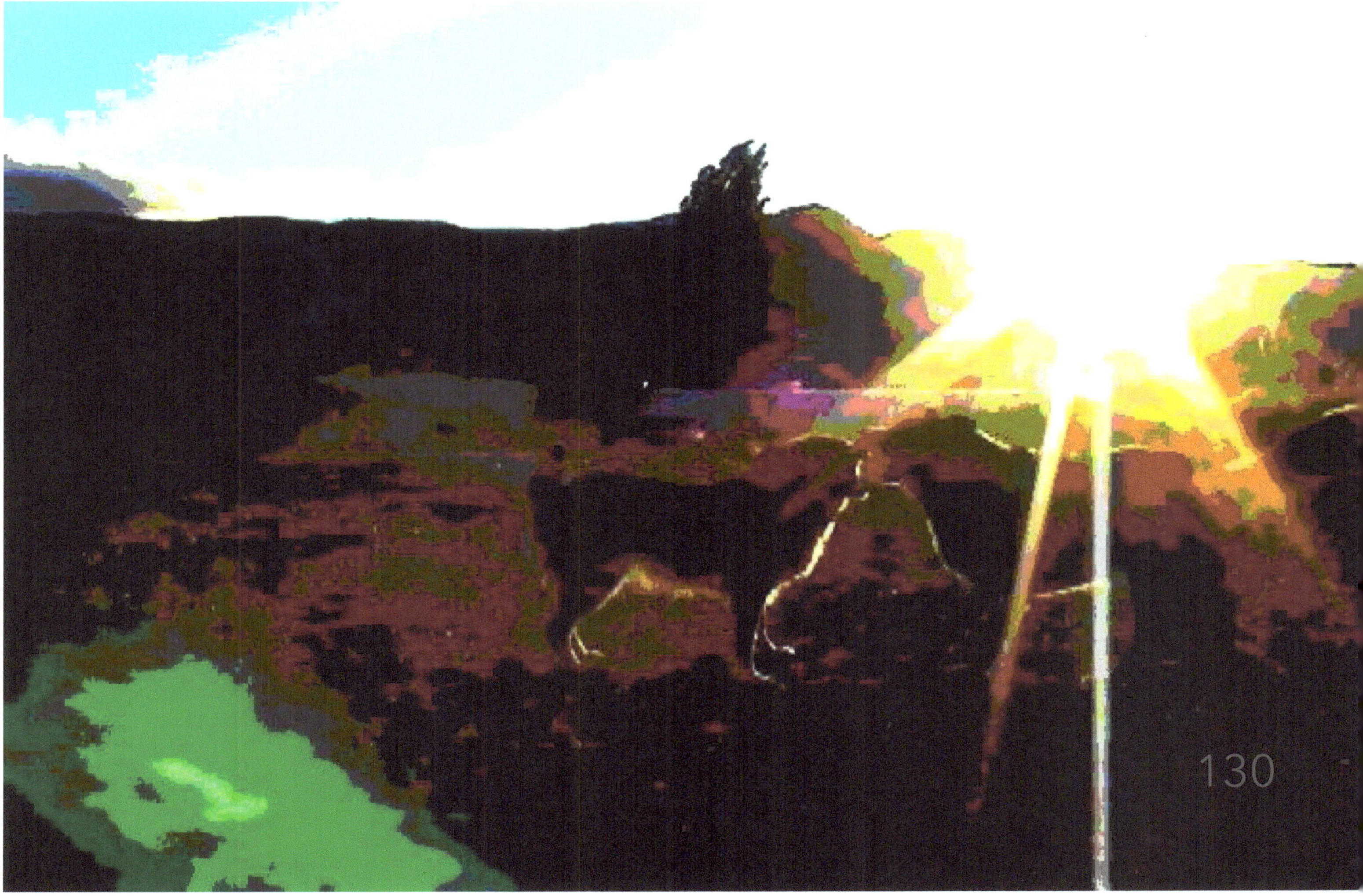

130

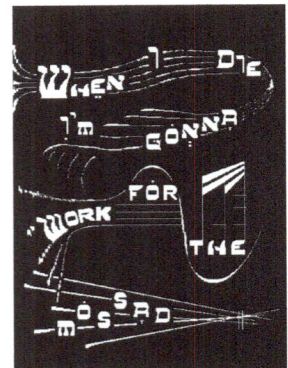
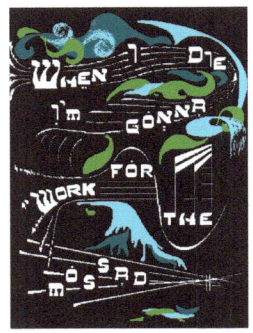
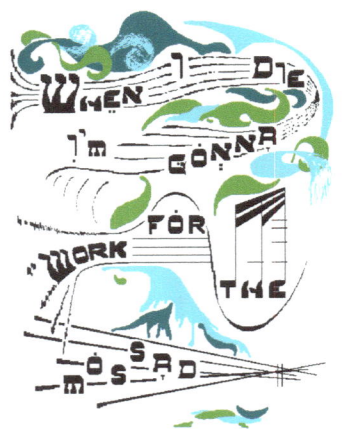
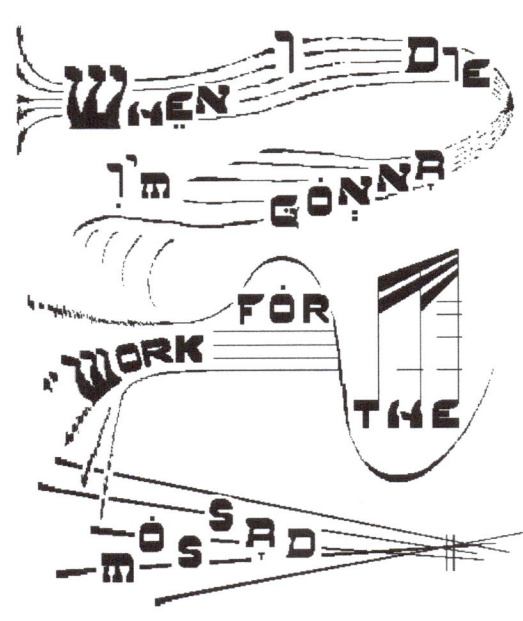

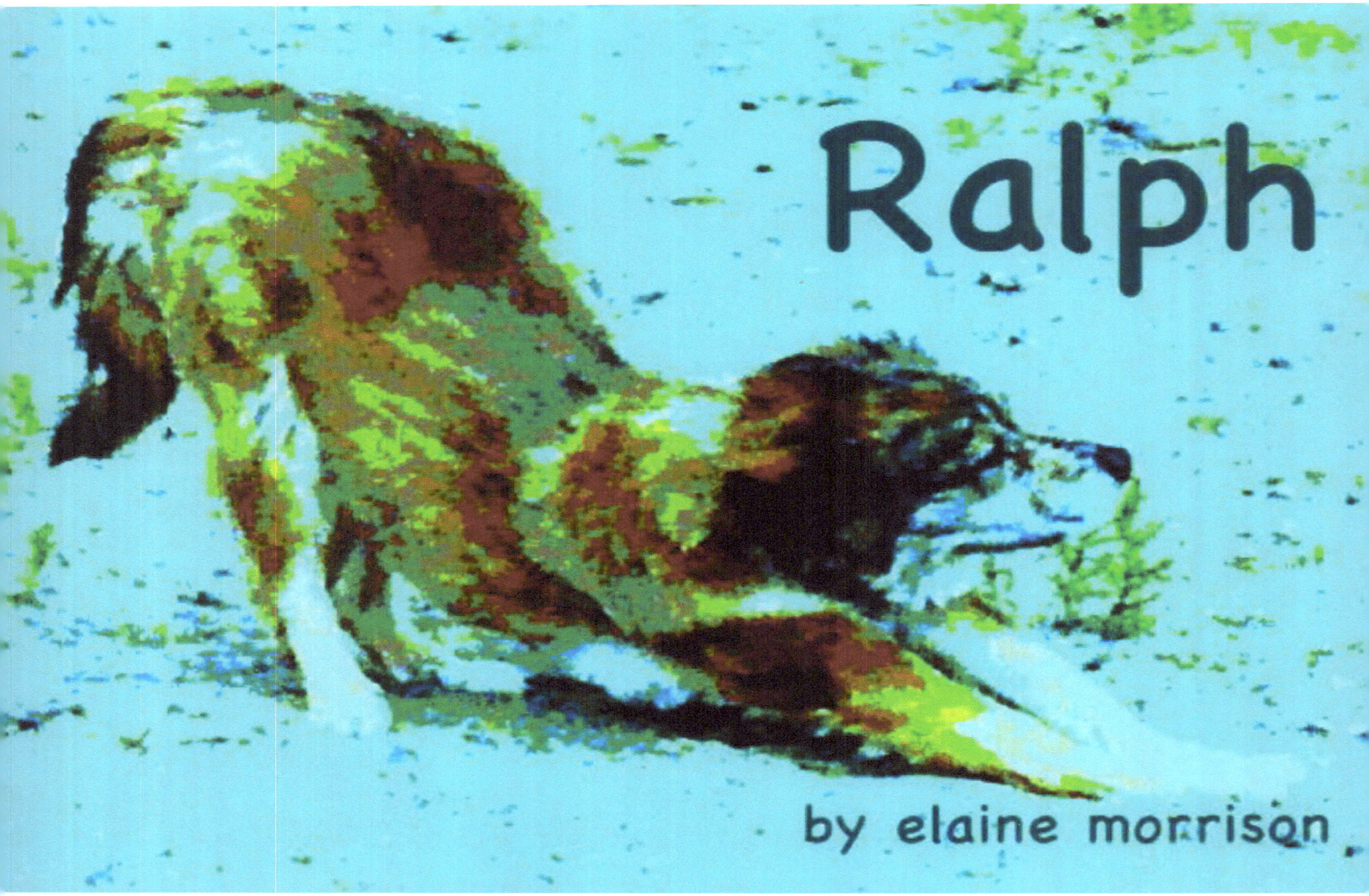

Ralph

by elaine morrison

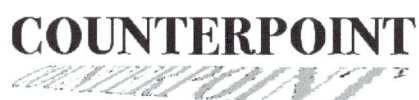
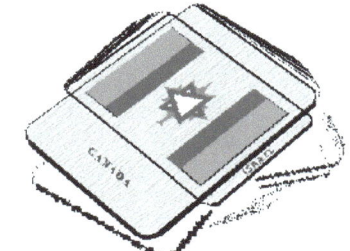

EVENT FIELD
BY ELAINE MORRISON

ZMAM

THE DRAFT

COUNTERPOINT

COUNTERPOINT

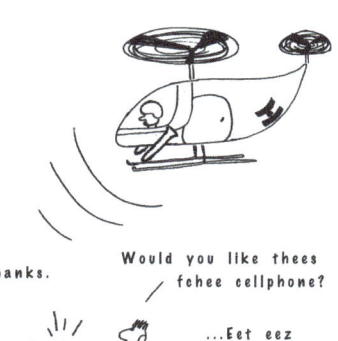
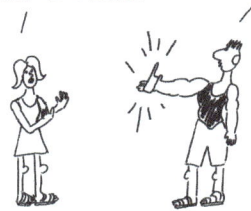

Uh, no thanks.

Would you like thees fchee cellphone?

...Eet eez fohr you.

The Draft

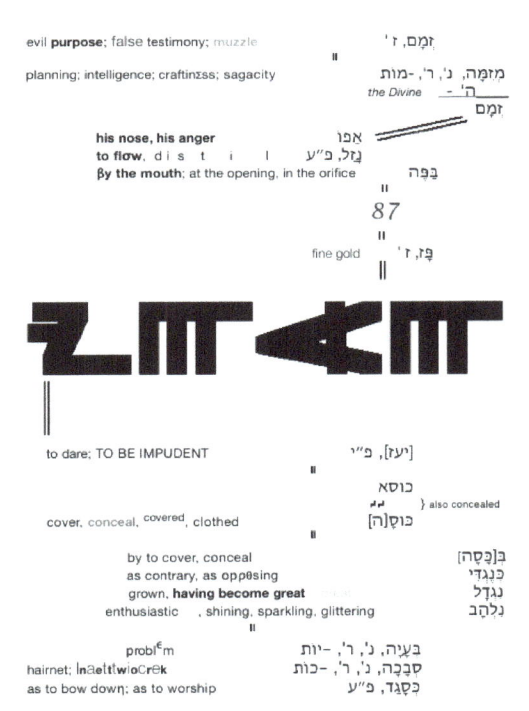

evil **purpose**; false testimony; muzzle   זְמָם, ז׳

planning; intelligence; craftin₂ss; sagacity   מְזִמָּה, נ׳, ר׳, -מוֹת
the Divine   ה׳ -

זְמָם

his nose, his anger   אַפּוֹ
to flow, d i s t i l   נָזַל, פ״ע
βy the mouth; at the opening, in the orifice   בַּפֶּה

87

fine gold   פָּז, ז׳

ZMAM

to dare; TO BE IMPUDENT   [יעז], פ״י

כוסא
} also concealed
cover, conceal, covered, clothed   כוֹסֶ[ה]

by to cover, conceal   בְּ[כַסָּה]
as contrary, as oppøsing   כְּנֶגְדִּי
grown, **having become great**   נִגְדַל
enthusiastic , shining, sparkling, glittering   נִלְהָב

probl€m   בְּעָיָה, נ׳, ר׳, -יוֹת
hairnet; ɪnæeltⅰwioⅭrɐk   סְבָכָה, נ׳, ר׳, -כוֹת
as to bow dowη; as to worship   כָּסַגַד, פ״ע

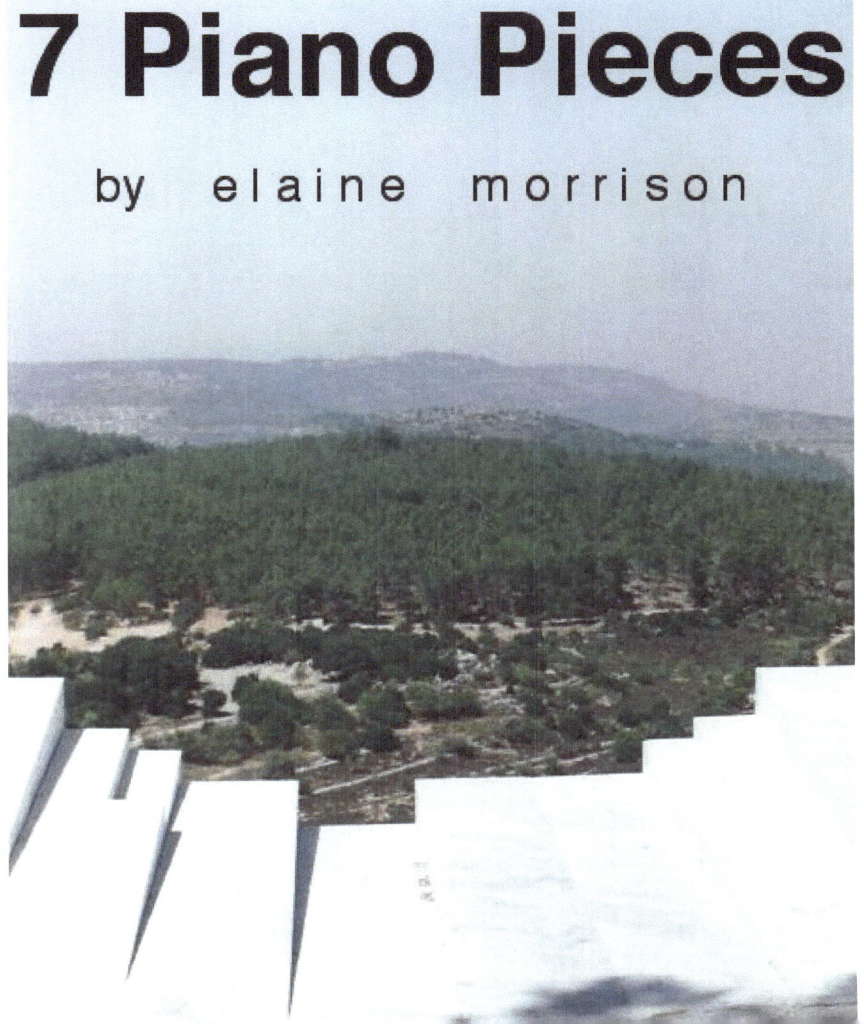

7 Piano Pieces
by elaine morrison